John Doyle is one of Australia's finest writers for stage and screen. His work spans the theatrical success of *The Pig Iron People* for the Sydney Theatre Company and *Vere (Faith)* for the State Theatre Company of South Australia, to the small screen acclaim of series such as *Changi*, *Marking Time* and *Two Men and a Tinnie* for the ABC.

He created the character of Roy Slaven in 1985, for ABC radio station Triple J. Since 1986, Roy has appeared alongside HG Nelson on various television series, including *Club Buggery*, *The Channel Nine Show*, *Win Roy and HG's Money*, *The Dream*, *The Monday Dump*, *The Ice Dream*, *The Cream*, *The Dream in Athens* and *The Memphis Trousers* and the long-running Sunday afternoon radio sports program *This Sporting Life* on Triple J.

In 2010, John was made a Member of the Order of Australia for his services to entertainment and as a supporter of charitable organisations such as the United Nations Children's Fund in Australia. John is Patron and a life governor of Autism Spectrum Australia.

Also by John Doyle

Books

This is the South Coast News and I'm Paul Murphy

Plays and Screenplays

Changi
The Pig Iron People
Vere (Faith)

Blessed

John Doyle

hachette
AUSTRALIA

hachette
AUSTRALIA

Published in Australia and New Zealand in 2021
by Hachette Australia
(an imprint of Hachette Australia Pty Limited)
Level 17, 207 Kent Street, Sydney NSW 2000
www.hachette.com.au

10 9 8 7 6 5 4 3 2 1

NATIONAL
LIBRARY
OF AUSTRALIA

A catalogue record for this
book is available from the
National Library of Australia

ISBN: 978 0 7336 4735 2 (paperback)

Cover and picture section design by Christabella Designs
Cover photograph courtesy of Alamy
Internal cricket and tennis images courtesy of Shutterstock
Internal chapter illustrations design by Bookhouse, Sydney
Typeset in 12.7/19.2 pt Bembo Std by Bookhouse, Sydney
Printed and bound in Great Britain by Clays Ltd, Elcograf S.p.A.

Dedicated to Deanna Doyle,
my partner since the age of twenty and whose skill with the
pencil and brush constantly excites and astounds me.

How the Adventure Began

I have known Roy all my life. When he called out of the blue with a plan to seriously focus on what he is calling his 'breakout year', I thought it was a terrific idea and offered him all the encouragement I could muster. The breakout year was 1967. I remember it well. I was there. He wanted his words in 'book form'. Fine, I thought. Good luck with it. He would have no trouble filling a book with his stories and feats of breathtaking skill.

Quite perversely, he wanted me to write it for him. I was most resistant. But he was dogged and did nothing but badger me for weeks. I agreed to assist on the understanding that he would do most, if not all, of the work. And I would accept the credit for its authorship.

He accepted that and we met up. It was good to see him. I was able to help in the remembering of some things, less certain with others. His recollection of the footy matches I saw him play that year, and the cricket matches and tennis matches we had together, are very accurate and align perfectly with my memory. To see him play in that year was to never forget him. He was an artist. His tennis was balletic. His cricket was full of grace. His football, sublime.

He had a couple of photos he had taken of our class. I have no memory of the photos being taken at all, but they helped bring back all sorts of forgotten incidents, both good and bad. However, he has, I think, let himself down by inventing things. Unnecessarily. The words he has put in my mouth, for example, are fanciful. But he insisted it was his story and he had the licence to 'call it as he saw it'.

We argued. He then said, without seeing the irony, that if I was to tell it as I saw it, it would be completely self-serving. And, as he had said, it was his story, not mine.

I stopped arguing and rolled the tape recorder, and for a few weeks I would see him for a few hours daily. I would delete my questions from the copy I'd faithfully written up, and let him read his own words. He would then, with a sharp pencil, make some changes – largely around 'tense' issues. For a bloke who showed little aptitude for English at school, he had become a real stickler for correct grammar.

The process of recording Roy's year of 1967 has revived our appreciation for Lithgow and Lithgow people. In the scheme of things, we realised that we had a rare and privileged upbringing. We both agree that it was lucky for us both that we got to know each other and became friends. We have been good for one another. I envy him his successes and his genius for being so gifted with anything that involves a moving ball. I still shake my head in disbelief whenever I hear him on the radio or see him on TV. In time, Lithgow Council will probably name a street after him.

I asked him if there was anything of my life he envied. He said, 'No, mate. Not a thing. Not a thing.' Would he ever swap places with me? He shook his head and laughed at me. He was being honest. And that's what I would say about Roy. His overwhelming hallmark is his honesty.

All the characters who appear in these recollections are real. Many are still living. I fear that Roy has been as fanciful in the words he has put in their mouths as well. Like me, I hope they are prepared to forgive him. The disturbing thing for me is, having read his book a few times now, I could be persuaded that everything might be true.

– John Doyle

Chapter One

'Young people need good teachers, like visible angels.'
SAINT JOHN BAPTIST, DE LA SALLE BROTHERS FOUNDER

'They can't run without legs.'
FATHER JOHN 'GRASSY' GRANNAL, LITHGOW SHAMROCKS COACH

'What do you take me for? A baboon?'
BROTHER HUGH CORCORAN, PRINCIPAL, DE LA SALLE, LITHGOW

Lithgow in summer often liked to surprise with a freezing day. Mercifully, Dean and Doyle had got to school early enough to get the fire going in the classroom.

Brother Connor appeared to be looking carefully at the details of the large sash window. He didn't appear to be interested in what view the window revealed. He hummed quietly. A tuneless hum.

Otherwise, the Third Form classroom was silent.

He then drew a deep breath and hummed one long note. He stopped when he was red in the face, turned and shouted, 'Time?'

Dean and Doyle put their hands up. 'Dean?'

Dean stood. 'Fifty-two seconds, Brother.'

'Doyle?'

Doyle stood. 'Fifty-three seconds, Brother.'

'Correct. We see eye to eye with time, do we not, Doyle?'

'We do, Brother.'

Dean and Doyle sat down.

'On your feet, Slaven.'

I stood. Brother Connor returned to his interest in the window frame.

The window was in good order. Closed, mercifully, the temperature outside being three degrees Celsius, thirty-eight degrees Fahrenheit, and Dean knew it in Kelvin. And it was windy. The wind came up through the floorboards of the classroom. The classroom was part of the original sandstone structure built in 1890 as an Anglican boarding school. On one side of the room was a fireplace, the row of desks beside it referred to as the Tropics. On the other side of the room was the Tundra. The fire was lit and tended to by the more responsible fellows – Dean, Doyle and O'Brien – regular members of the Tropics. Crawlers, basically.

The Tundra was inhabited by myself, Brennan, Benson, Flynn, Hall and Brewer. There were ten others in the Temperate Zone – Mills, Wall, Dowd, Marsland, Lennan and company.

Brother Connor was a dapper man whose black soutane and prominent white starched collar were pressed and neat. He hummed with his hands in his pockets, one clutching a bespoke, finely stitched, burnished, laminated leather waddy that poked out as a stiff cock might, albeit off-centre.

He turned and fixed me in his gaze. He stopped humming.

'Slaven,' he said. 'Tell me why I should be interested in triangles.'

Brother Connor liked to set traps. His pleasure came from embarrassing us. And in giving him the slightest reason to get out his waddy and deliver either one or two cuts across the hand. He was by any measure a weird bloke. I took my time. 'Umm . . .'

'Don't mumble, boy. Well?'

Silence, then giggles from Benson and Brewer.

'Lord help us, Slaven. Dean?'

Dean stood. A large fellow. 'Triangulation can be used to establish the height of an object, Brother.'

Brother Connor nodded. 'Now, Slaven, how might Dean here establish the height of the northern wall of the academy through triangulation?'

'Umm . . . he'd probably eat the triangle, Brother, climb the northern wall and jump off, getting Doyle to measure the time it took to hit the ground. Work it out from that.'

Giggles from Brewer. And Brennan. And Benson.

'Quite the wit today, Slaven. Describe a triangle for me.'

'Three-sided figure, Brother.'

'Indeed it is. Sit down, Slaven. On your feet, Benson.'

Benson stood.

Brother Connor continued. 'Doyle, if I was a betting man, what odds would you give Benson here answering a question correctly about our friend, the triangle?'

Doyle stood. 'Depends on the degree of difficulty, Brother. You could well frame a question that no one could answer.'

Brother Connor looked heavenward, smiling with amusement. 'Good point, Doyle. And well made. Therefore I want you to frame both the question and the market.'

Doyle thought. 'Name a type of triangle is the question. One to four the odds.'

Brother Connor thought about this. 'An eighty per cent chance of you getting this right, Benson. Doyle here has more confidence in you than I have. Well, Benson? Name a type of triangle.'

Benson drew breath. He knew he was out of his depth. 'Does it have to be big or small, Brother?'

Brother Connor looked stunned. Then burst into laughter. 'Benson, I don't know what rabbit hole your deliciously damaged mind is taking us down, but I'm intrigued.' He closed in on Benson. 'Big interests me.'

Benson looked relieved. He said confidently, 'A sphinx, Brother.'

Laughter.

The bell rang. Brother Connor took out his strap and approached Doyle.

'On your feet, Doyle. Left hand.' Doyle held out his left hand.

'Those odds were unacceptable. You will guarantee Benson can name three types of triangle tomorrow. Understood?'

'Yes, Brother.'

Brother Connor brought down the strap across Doyle's fingers. He flinched in pain.

'Dismissed.'

I quite enjoyed seeing someone from the Tropics getting the strap. Getting the cuts was as common as shivering in the Tundra. It amused Brother Connor to occasionally give a crawler the cuts. Kept them from being too up themselves, which they were prone to be. It was rare to see Doyle having to hold out his hand. He hated it. He was angry. Close to tears, he blew his hand and packed his port one-handed.

The Brothers lived in the old building. The principal was Brother Hugh, a bloke who had two gears – benign weirdo or red-faced bellowing autocrat. Hard to put an age on him, maybe forty-five or so. His favourite saying was 'What do you take me for? A baboon?' Oddly enough, in certain light, he looked exactly like a baboon.

Brother Hubert was ancient. Tall, with shocking arthritis in his hands and all the hallmarks of some sort of senile decline. He often had a stalactite of snot, which dangled before attaching itself to his chin, whereupon it was wiped away by a large white handkerchief. He took us for English.

Rounding out the brotherhood was Brother Michael, a fit, young, friendly bloke who played tennis with Dean and Doyle and me on occasion. He was too young to be seriously feared and I think he found it easier to make friends with the students than the weirdos he had to live with.

There were two lay teachers – they lived together in a small house near the tech on the other side of town. Jack Connolly was sixty and smelled of the tobacco he kept in his pipe, which was either in his hand, in his mouth, or in the top pocket of his brown tweed jacket. He was of florid complexion and had hairs of different colours growing in the middle of his nose. He was the woodwork/metalwork specialist. His housemate was Harold. Harold was in his early thirties, fit, but with vague suggestions of a drug habit and assorted lifestyle issues. Geography was his go. Harold could be embarrassingly intimate.

'Funny thing, boys. Jack hasn't a clue. The package arrives from Sydney. Early. He's up. I'm not. He hasn't a clue. I had to run down bloody Mort Street in my underpants. He hasn't a clue. I was . . . yeah. Jack. Anyway . . .'

Harold would focus. Be disappointed in himself. 'Where was I, Doyle?'

'The savannah, Sir.'

It's 1967. In Lithgow.

•

People who visited Lithgow described it not as 'the glorious Gateway to the Central West', but as the Arsehole of the Universe. They probably only saw it when it was insanely hot, which it often was in summer; or when it was bitterly cold, which it mostly was in winter. The architecture wasn't fabulous – fibro homes beside rows of semi-detached Victorian miners' quarters, with a few Federation brick piles scattered throughout. Generally speaking, the brick homes used a particular depression-inducing brick that was probably locally produced.

To anyone driving though the town in July, when the fierce westerly was blowing and the sleet was in the air, it would have indeed seemed like the Arsehole of the Universe. Especially had they stopped and looked at the clothing and bedsheets blowing on backyard clotheslines. Specks of black coal dust created lines of grey stains down every item. The visitor would have breathed in a rich atmosphere, with every chimney pushing out thick streams of black smoke. Hogarth would have been drawn to etch every street and lane.

To me, it was beautiful. It was home. I had no desire to live anywhere else. Ever. There was a communal enjoyment in meeting the town's challenges. And when the sun shone and the wind held its breath, in the nooks of the finger valleys and the ridges that ringed them was to be found sublime, glorious pristine beauty. Wallaby, kangaroo, wombat, parrot, echidna, kookaburra, magpie, currawong in eucalypt forests that stretched forever.

It was a coal mining town, an iron and steel making town and then an arms manufacturing city. Most importantly, it was a town that appreciated sport. Cricket had A-grade and B-grade competitions, Rugby League was played at first-grade level, reserve grade, under twenty-ones, under eighteens and under sixteens. Hockey was played in two grades, basketball in two grades and the council provided tennis courts for free. Squash was popular. As was netball. And swimming. And bowls. And snooker. And the greyhounds. And Marjorie Jackson was our most famous champion, being the fastest runner on the planet for four years in the 1950s. Barry Rushworth was our greatest Rugby League player – he toured with the Australian Kangaroos. And Nancy Hill was a member of the Australian Women's Basketball team.

I was always active. I loved competition. Loved competing with blokes at anything. And loved being in a team. And I didn't mind the freezing cold. Or the heat. I could play sport all year round. So, Lithgow was made for me.

•

De La Salle Academy was a boys-only school. It was on the outskirts of town in the suburb of Littleton. Saint Patrick's was the Catholic girls' school and it sat in the middle of town beside Saint Patrick's Church, the presbytery and Saint Joseph's Convent. We'd see the girls every first Friday at a mass held at midday. We'd travel by either bus or bike. The bike riders would arrive first and show off in front of the girls who gathered outside the church under the steely supervision of the nuns, dressed in their imposing brown habits. I preferred to take the bus. Blokes who rode ended up sweaty and looking like dicks.

Flynn rode once. He was showing off in front of the girls when his foot slipped off the pedal, causing his scrotum to collide with the bike's crossbar. This inflicted great pain, and the trouser cuff of his right dangling leg got caught up in the chain and then into the sprocket. He and his bike collapsed sideways into the gutter. While the combined schools roared with laughter, three girls we knew came to his assistance. Barbara, Deirdre and Anne. He never rode to mass again.

When the bus arrived we'd line up and Brother Connor would take charge. I liked to sit where I could see the girls. One I looked out for in particular. Susan Morgan. I was in love with her. We had bonded at a footy match last season. I'd seen her with her sister and two other girls watching the game from near the sideline. We were defending against the Lithgow High under sixteens and I saw a terrific opportunity – one of their players, Mark Wilkinson, had made a break down the sideline. I was in cover and lined him up to time the tackle so I'd be right in front of Susan. I timed it pretty well and cut his legs out from under him, but hit my nose on his knee, breaking it. Blood everywhere.

The referee was Wayne Hammond's dad. Mr Hammond stopped the match, looked at my nose and said, 'It's a clean break, Roy, which is a good thing.' He looked at the horrified Susan and her group, noticed she was eating a Paddle Pop, and asked her to quickly finish it. Then he took the stick, wiped it on my shorts, snapped it in two and shoved a half up each of my nostrils to re-centre my nose. Hurt like fuck. 'Keep your head back for a few minutes. You'll have to go off.'

I left the field. I looked at Susan and thanked her for her stick. She told me to do what Mr Hammond had said to do.

So I lay down not far from the sideline and she sat with me. I learnt that she was a bit of a swot, was good at Maths and hated Rugby League.

'What about cricket?' I asked.

'Pretty boring.'

'Tennis?'

'Sometimes.'

'What's your favourite song?'

'"Eleanor Rigby".'

'What about "Friday On My Mind"?'

She was in two minds.

'It's the best song ever written.'

She grinned. 'No. Not a chance.'

At that point Brother Connor arrived on the scene. The game was over and we had won. He wore his suit with dog collar. Hands in pockets, he paused to drink in the scene.

'Well, well, well. How sweet is this, Slaven? A perfect tableau of the Crimean War. A fallen soldier and Nurse Nightingale in attendance. And it's an heroic story. An important tackle, Slaven. An act of bravery. Susan Morgan, isn't it?'

'Yes, Brother.'

He looked at her closely. 'Remember, Susan Morgan, a young woman is measured by the company she keeps.'

Then Mr Hammond joined us. He bent down and took my head in his hands. He examined my nose and nodded his approval. 'It'll be as right as rain in three weeks. Leave the sticks in for a couple of days, then tug 'em out. Okay?' I nodded. 'Well played, young fella.' He nodded to Brother Connor and walked off.

I stood up, Susan's sister and mates joined us, and Brother Connor said he'd drive me home in the old Humber Hawk the Brothers were starting to find unreliable. But we had bonded, me and Susan Morgan. The opportunities to see her were few. Mass, however, was one.

•

Mass could be pretty dull. Never an exciting show, and made worse on this particular day with the ritual being suspended for the first time for some singing of 'Kumbaya' by Sister Francis and her haltingly strummed nylon-stringed acoustic guitar. She was joined by the three Cullen girls. Boring as buggery. Mind you, she would have made 'Friday On My Mind' as boring as buggery as well. I liked music, but what Sister Francis produced wasn't music. It was anti-music. It was as if she had a mission to kill music. I caught Susan's eye during the performance and mimed a yawn. She laughed. The exchange was seen by both Brother Connor and Sister Pius.

The only other thing of note from that mass was that at the end of the sermon — can't remember a thing about it but it did go on — Doyle, who was one of the three altar boys, fell over because his right leg had gone dead. A few of us laughed. I could see he felt like shit, because he looked stupid. He limped delivering the cruets.

I had auditioned to be an altar boy at the same time as Doyle, Dean, Brewer, O'Brien and Flynn. It had taken place in the front room of the presbytery when we were in fourth class in primary school. Father Whelan did the audition in his final year as parish priest. He was a tall, ancient man with an Irish accent. He said he was looking for boys who 'had the head for the Latin'. He was also looking for boys whose parents could afford the cost of the vestments – a red surplice and white soutane, red slippers and a starched collar held together with a brass stud. While I had the head, things were a bit challenged at home and forking out money for the costume was quickly ruled out. Dad's work at the Genders coal mine had come to an end and he had been relying on seasonal shearing work, which was sporadic and unreliable.

It was at the start of the year I started Third Form that Dad left permanently. Mum got some shiftwork at Berlei's, which she hated, so much of the time I pretty well had the house to myself.

The house was fibro with two bedrooms and had been painted a light green inside and out sometime in the 1940s. All the floors were linoleum apart from the laundry out the back, which was concrete. Dad had made most of the furniture, which had a distinctive solid style. Mum had made a lot of cushions, which made most of the seating really comfortable. And while the kitchen was sparse, the stove worked well even though the oven didn't. My room had a three-quarter bed, a chest of three drawers and a broomstick Dad had nailed across the picture railing in the corner to use for hanging clothes. Home was very comfortable. Freezing, though, in winter. In summer it could become an oven.

Anyway, it didn't worry me too much not being an altar boy. Generally speaking, altar boys were crawlers. Tropics types. With the exception of Brewer. He was a rare breed being the only altar boy in the Tundra. He had a terrific imagination. His composition 'A Day in the Life of a Penny' was the stuff of legend. He read it out in class. When the penny ended up in Brother Hubert's underpants, the class was on the floor in stitches. The room roared. The ancient Brother, who was also known as Sherb, laughed his head off. He grabbed Brewer gently by the ears and kissed the top of his head. Sherb was proud of him.

But Brewer sometimes just couldn't shut up. That's how he ended up in the Tundra. He used to nick some of the altar wine and sell it to interested parties. There were two types: standard and super. Super was wine that had been blessed by the priest. How he got it, I don't know. Standard was out of the bottle, not out of the cruet. A cruet was what the priests called a small glass jug. Wine and water were delivered to the priest in cruets during mass just before the consecration. Brewer sold it from rinsed Fanta bottles. I bought five cents' worth of standard. It was sweet and was just the thing to have on a cold day – it would warm you up. I really liked it. But once was enough. Special was twice the price. Never tried it. Brennan did. He thought it was stronger. Brewer kept this up for a couple of months, so he could easily afford a top-shelf genuine Russell yoyo when they became the rage later that year. Then the supply dried up. He wasn't caught, but one of the priests must have noticed the rate at which the wine was disappearing. Pretty much whatever happened in the sacristy was a mystery to me, as mysterious as transubstantiation or the need of the word cruet.

And the mass was changing. It was suddenly a post-Vatican II world. There was an attempt to make the mass more accessible. This meant the Latin was no longer being used and the priest, for the first time, faced the congregation during the consecration, so that what used to appear as mysterious no longer had much mystery at all. In addition, the priest was now asking the congregation to turn to each other and offer a 'sign of peace'. Most of us hated that. Some of the men, like Mr Goggin, would turn and stretch out his hand to as many people as he could reach, clutch and say with an enthusiastic grin, 'Peace be with you.' It forced you to make contact with people you didn't know. I think I caught a cold from Mrs Cullen in the pew in front of me, when she turned and sneezed in my face as she tried to say 'Peace be with you.' Mum then got the cold from me. The whole confection was just embarrassing.

Embarrassing, too, was the introduction of members of the congregation reading the epistle from the pulpit. Mr Seaton earned sniggers because of his stutter, which made his stutter worse. Sometimes his performance took twelve minutes. O'Brien timed it. Palpable relief from us all when he stepped away and tiptoed by the altar on his way to rejoining us. It must have been his penance. Father Keogh's idea, probably. And Mr Mierzac's English was so poor that no one had a clue what he was saying. It might as well have been Latin.

But the most embarrassing thing by a mile was bringing the acoustic guitar into the church. It encouraged the largely untalented player to bring the result of hundreds of hours of unschooled practice out of the bedroom, where it should have stayed.

The guitar was used as an uplifting distraction while the Holy Communion was being received. Often the communion would be well and truly finished while we listened to the Cullen sisters' recent additions to their set list. The Seekers generally supplied their material. 'A World of Our Own' sadly failed to get the congregation singing along, despite enthusiastic encouragement from the Cullen sisters to do so. After a month, they were told to limit it to two songs only. Not eight.

•

Sister Pius apparently gave Susan Morgan a fearful dressing-down for giggling during 'Kumbaya'. And Brother Connor gave me four cuts. I didn't mind. It was a small price to pay for having a genuine contact with the girl of my dreams, and not long after I found out where she lived – in Enfield Avenue, Littleton. It wasn't far from the academy. Littleton wasn't the only suburb of Lithgow. There were a few others. Oaky Park. McKellars Park. The Vale of Clwyyd. Most of the streets around

Littleton had names associated with either World Wars or armaments. Bayonet Street, Passchendale Street, Rifle Parade, Suvla Street, Fallen Digger Lane, Lone Pine Avenue, Tobruk Street, Carbine Street, Amiens Street, Bren Street, Ordnance Avenue and Pozieres Street. Our school was in Rabaul Street. Dean lived in Ordnance Avenue and Doyle in Martini Parade.

Brother Connor to Doyle. 'Doyle. Martini Parade. Martini. Who was Martini? Any idea?'

Doyle was quick to reply. 'A hero, Brother. The first Anzac to fall.'

Brother Connor was quite moved. 'Really?' He returned to his ritual examination of the window frame. Doyle stayed standing. There was silence but for currawongs.

'Where was Martini born, Doyle?'

'Italy, Brother.'

'Italy's a big place. Can you be more specific?'

Currawongs.

'Assisi, I think, Brother.'

'Assisi? Just like Saint Francis.'

'Yes, Brother.'

'And how did he come to be an Anzac?'

'Family migrated.'

Brother Connor nodded. 'Catholic?'

'Of course, Brother.'

'And settled in Lithgow?'

Doyle nodded.

'Trade?'

'Furniture-maker, Brother.'

Brother Connor pondered. Then, 'On your knees, boys.' We all slid off our seats and knelt. 'We're going to offer up a prayer for Martini of Assisi.' Then he reconsidered. 'Although, strictly speaking, as an Anzac, he should be Martini of Lithgow, don't you think, Doyle?'

'Yes, Brother.'

I said, 'Shouldn't he be Martini of Littleton?'

Brother Connor went off. 'Slaven, you are an idiot and a worm. What is Slaven, Benson?'

'An idiot and a worm, Brother.'

'Yes. And you'd know, Benson. Let us pray. Hail Mary, full of grace . . .'

Three weeks later, Doyle got four. Brother Connor had told the Martini story at some fundraiser for the Catholic Youth Club and been laughed at. Martini, apparently, was an Englishman who had designed and manufactured rifles.

'Honestly, Brother, it's what I was told.'

'Why don't I believe you?'

'I don't know, Brother.'

Brother Connor gripped his waddy with white knuckles. I had never seen him more angry. He began to shout. 'Who told you?'

'Alan, Brother.'

'Alan? Historian is he? Of note? Alan?'

'I don't think so, Brother.

'Who is he? Who is Alan?'

'He's my uncle, Brother.'

Brother Connor almost writhed with anger. His whole body was involved.

'When? When did he tell you?' He was close to tears of rage.

Then Doyle said, 'Last Christmas, Brother. He made a fool of me, too, Brother.'

'Doyle, Doyle, Doyle, there is something that doesn't smell right. Did anyone else witness this story of Uncle Alan's?'

'The whole family, Brother.'

Brother Connor paced for a time. Then stopped and smiled. 'We have a telephone now, boys. In the house.' He propped beside Doyle. 'Is there a telephone in the Doyle household?'

Doyle showed signs of fear. I think we all knew where this was going.

'Yes, Brother.'

'Doyle, you have a choice here. I am going to set the class an exercise, and we are going to go and telephone your mother and have this story confirmed here and now. If it is not confirmed you will receive six and be further punished for being known at home to have lied to a member of the order of Saint John Baptist. Clearly a sin. A mortal sin. If you confirm with me now that the story is of your invention, then you will receive four. The thing is, Doyle, you take things too far.'

Doyle had form in getting teachers into trouble. I respected him for this. The year before, Dean had written a play for some competition the library was throwing. It came second. It was a short piece, in which a murder is solved by a shrewd detective. The top three plays were put on in the Lithgow High auditorium one Thursday night. I went along. Doyle was playing the detective. All the Brothers were present, and quite a few family members and members of the public. There would have been a hundred people all up. The curtain lifts, and there is Doyle with a pipe. He had tobacco in it and lit it and smoked throughout the performance. He used the pipe for gesturing and what have you. I can't remember a thing about the play. But I remember the pipe. There were a lot of laughs, but I noticed that Brother Connor was furious that a boy would be smoking so boldly in public. A De La Salle boy. He glared at young Brother Michael, who was the man in charge of the production.

There was a scene in the car park later as the Brothers loaded into the Humber Hawk. Young Brother Michael was sent to Coventry. The pipe-smoking Doyle went unpunished on this occasion.

Brother Connor savoured the four he gave Doyle for the Martini incident. He insisted all be on the left hand and waited five minutes between each blow. Doyle stood in painful anticipation for most of the period.

Chapter Two

'One penny, one cent, two pennies two cents,
three pennies two cents, too.'
<small>DECIMAL CURRENCY JINGLE</small>

'You are a worm and no man.'
<small>BROTHER HUGH CORCORAN</small>

I wasn't unhappy Dad had left. Dad could be trouble. He didn't seem to like many people. He was tall and well built. Dark hair. Handsome. He taught me how to tackle. 'It's all about where you put your head. Keep your head away from his hip. Use your shoulder. Your shoulder, his ribs. If he's getting away, dive at his knees.' I never saw Dad and Mum being affectionate. They competed. He was stronger; she was smarter.

Mum and me would sometimes watch Dad playing footy and Mum would often give him an earful after the game. 'Honestly, Bob, you deserved to lose. You are always running the wrong way. Even Roy could see that. There are ten blokes on this side and two on the other, so what do you do? Run at the ten. Every time. You don't think.'

Dad would swallow the match review in silence.

On my eighth birthday I was given a brand-new football and Dad and I got mucking about in the backyard, playing touch footy. It was fun. Mum watched. Mum got me aside and showed me how to wrong-foot him. It was so easy. I'd feign one direction and head off in the other. I started running around him with ease. Mum was laughing and Dad got really competitive. He ended the game by tackling me with full force. It winded me and I was really dazed. I had to go straight to bed. Mum screamed at him. 'For God's sake, Bob! It's touch footy! He's eight years old!'

Everyone else called him 'Bot'. Bot Slaven. They called him Bot because he was always botting smokes from blokes at the Commercial Hotel or the Workmen's Club, where he spent a fair bit of his time. For a time I was 'Bot's boy'. I hated it. Mercifully, it was short lived. Thorley called me Bot's boy once. Thorley was a Temperate Zone lightweight. I thought about punching his head in. But instead, I stood very close to him and said, 'Mates call me Roy, Thorley. Deadshits call me other things.' He nodded. And that was that. A couple of Dad's drinking mates kept calling me Bot's boy, but I didn't see them very often and it disappeared.

It was a typical January when Dad left. Hot as buggery.

Just after New Year's Day, Dad's brother Uncle Baz and his wife, Aunty Rita, arrived to stay the night. They'd driven up from Cowra. Dad had forgotten to tell Mum and we didn't have any bedding prepared for them. Mum really had the shits. Dad went over to Doyle's corner shop for something for tea and bought a case of Resch's Dinner Ale. 'Dirty Annie,' Uncle Baz called it.

Meanwhile Mum and I changed the sheets on my bed and she told me I'd have to sleep out on the bags. We had a stack of potato sacks in the backyard beside the coal heap. I'd lay them out on the concrete and put a sheet on them and, with a pillow, I'd make do. It wasn't great but it was what it was and I liked Baz and Rita. The house was like a furnace anyway. All the windows were open but it was a lot hotter inside than out. I was happy to sleep outside in the end. Mum ratted around in the kitchen and Baz talked family stuff and Aunty Rita was really embarrassed and gave Uncle Baz odd looks.

Baz looked like Dad. He was a bit older, a bit bigger and he had smile lines around his eyes. Dad had no smile lines. Dad didn't smile much at all. Rita looked and dressed like a film star. Mum liked her. And Mum liked Baz.

Eventually we sat down at the table. Mum had assembled some sliced tomato on a plate with vinegar drizzled over it, celery chopped up on another plate, a tin of sliced beetroot in a bowl, an opened tin of baked beans and Dad had bought a stack of sliced devon and a loaf of tank top white bread. He forgot the butter. With the tomato sauce, I thought it was all pretty good, but Mum hardly touched anything, although she drank the beer. Dad had put a few bottles in the fridge, but they weren't ready yet in his opinion and he was furious with Mum because she'd knocked the top off a warm one. 'You're wasting it!'

We ate on in silence. Dad repeated himself as Mum threw a whole glass back. 'You're fucking wasting it!'

Uncle Baz, never a man for the swearing, had a word to Dad. 'No need for that word, Bob. Come on, mate, it's mixed company.'

Dad measured this. Mum poured herself another glass of DA. Aunty Rita said, 'I don't mind beer warm.' Mum poured her a glass. Rita toasted Mum. Uncle Baz then said that he could easily drink a room temperature beer, like they do in England. He'd been to England with a Kangaroo Rugby League tour in the fifties. He never got to play in a test match, much to his regret.

I could tell Dad was really getting the hump. Usually when he got like that, I disappeared. I'd leave them to it. It usually ended up with Mum in tears and Dad going to the Commercial or the club. This time, I stayed.

'Oh, yeah, we had many a warm beer in Hull. Wonderful people, Yorkshire people, really generous.'

I loved it when Uncle Baz talked about his tour to England, but Dad didn't. Dad sat back. He considered, swallowed the last bit of his devon and tomato sauce sandwich, and spoke. 'This is my house. This is not Yorkshire. It's the middle of summer and I will not have warm beer drunk in this house.'

Mum said, 'Too late,' and threw back a mouthful theatrically.

I laughed. Uncle Baz laughed and said to Mum, 'Pour us one, Paulette.'

Dad stood. 'What did I just fucking say?' He grabbed Mum's bottle.

Uncle Baz stood up, leaned over the table and grabbed the bottle of beer out of Dad's grip. He poured the last of it into a glass and threw it back. 'That's delicious. We might need another bottle, Paulette.'

'We've got plenty.' Mum stood.

I watched Dad. He knew what was going to happen. He knew Baz was going to hit him if he wasn't careful. He went to the fridge and pulled a bottle from the freezer. 'This one's cold enough,' he said, and the drama disappeared. On the surface. I knew Mum and Dad had unfinished business.

They went through quite a few bottles of beer. I asked Baz who was the best he'd ever played with. He said, 'Norm. Norm Provan. A real leader. Tough. He'd lift everyone else.' He then looked at me closely. 'I'm hearing terrific things about you, young fella. Ron Livermore was talking about you.' I didn't know Ron Livermore. 'He's a state selector for the under eighteens. He watched you playing in the grand final last year. Said you had something special. You and the O'Brien kid.'

It was the Christmas present I'd never received. Then he went out to his car and brought in an Australian jersey wrapped in brown paper. He said, 'This is for you, Roy. It's one I wore in a tour match against Bradford.' He handed it to me. I unwrapped it. It was the most precious thing I had ever seen.

Or touched. 'Norm was in the team. And Clive Churchill. Bloody good team it was.'

I was speechless. I couldn't believe it was mine. I got a bit teary.

Rita put her arms around me, saying, 'Oh, look at him, Baz, he's overwhelmed.'

Baz had a long pull of his beer. 'Mark my words,' he said, 'there will come a day when a kid will be just as overwhelmed to touch a jersey Roy Slaven wore in a test match.' And Mum smiled.

Even Dad had a good look at it. 'What would it be worth?' he asked.

'Priceless,' said Rita. And Mum nodded.

I took it to my room and carefully put it away.

There was a scene that night. I missed it because I was out on the bags. But I was woken by loud voices. It seemed Dad had had a go at Mum, and Uncle Baz had intervened. Whatever happened, Mum ended up with a black eye and Dad had taken the Holden and gone. Later, I discovered he'd taken my Australian Rugby League jersey, so I was as upset as Mum was.

Uncle Baz and Aunty Rita left the next morning. They had some things to do in Sydney. Their son Kerry had polio and he was getting some sort of treatment at some hospital there. Kerry wore callipers. He'd never be able to play Rugby League. We learnt later that Dad had taken himself out west to a place called Caragabal and was shearing there. It would be years before I saw him again. Never saw the jersey again.

•

Not having Dad about changed the mood of the house. It was much better. Mum was down in the dumps for a while and her mood wasn't helped when Father Keogh would call in, giving her advice and support. He'd make a point of dropping in every Wednesday. He was a bit hard to understand with his Irish brogue. He was an ugly bloke to look at. Would sometimes dribble a bit when speaking. Had shocking teeth.

'And have you written to your husband at all, Mrs Slaven?'

'I haven't an address, Father. I could try Bob Slaven, Thoughtless Street, Knuckletown, I suppose. Might get to him.'

Father Keogh took a crumpled white handkerchief from his pocket and wiped his chin.

'Have you prayed for his return?'

'Can't say I have, Father.'

Then he'd play with his crucifix.

'A boy should have his father about, don't you think?'

'In an ideal world, Father, but it's not an ideal world.'

'Well then, let's all pray now, eh? Pray for his return. A decade of the rosary.'

Mum looked at him squarely. 'I don't have the time, Father. I'm due at the factory in an hour and I've got the ironing to get done.'

'Mrs Slaven, there should always be time for prayer.'

'I know there should be, Father, but today there isn't.'

Father Keogh tut-tutted and headed for the door.

'Well, I'll pray for you, Mrs Slaven.'

'Good. Thank you, Father.'

Then Mum turned to me. 'Thought he'd never leave.'

•

I never really understood how the chemistry between Mum and Dad worked. I know my birthday is close to their wedding anniversary. They had their tenth when I was ten. I'm fifteen now and Mum's thirty-two. Shotgun marriage, they call it. And it was a mixed marriage. Mum wasn't a Catholic when she met Dad. But I really liked Mum. When she was happy, she had a smile that could light up a city. And she was smart. She didn't finish school but was great at working things out. She had a sewing machine and made her own dresses. She helped me with homework. She was actually disappointed when I didn't have homework.

Mum had been teaching herself how to type for a while. Mrs Leslie, a neighbour, had lent her a typewriter and a typewriting textbook and she'd spend a couple of hours a day practising. Sometimes I would dictate. She could type fifty words a minute. Her dream was to be accepted into the typing pool at the Small Arms Factory. I think she needed to be able to do eighty.

We rarely saw Mum's family. She was born in Portland, a cement-producing town half an hour's drive away and most of the family still lived there, but because she'd become a Catholic, she'd been ostracised by them all.

The facts are that Mum and Dad met at the Festival of The Valley Gymkhana, in the spring of 1952. Dad was in the marathon – twice around the showground, then the climb up Scotsman's Hill, back down and another lap of the showground. Mum liked the look of him and put two shillings on him – a fair bit back then. He won by seven minutes. Suddenly she had five pounds – a small fortune. She spoke to Dad and offered to buy him a drink. He had a car. Nine months later, I'm born.

•

Mum could have coached Rugby League. She gave me better advice than Brother Hugh ever did. Or Brother Connor. She taught me how to read a game: to look at the numbers, who's where, where we could make an overlap, when to run and when not to, when to pass, how to pass, and to practise, practise, practise. She invented the torpedo pass. 'It's all in the wrist,' she'd say. And we'd sometimes spend an hour in the backyard passing the footy to each other. Brother Hugh was incredibly impressed with the torpedo pass. He was our main coach. And our Religious Knowledge teacher. And, as I said, he was the school principal.

'Eyes on me, men. All eyes, Flynn. You are going to watch Slaven pass me the ball. Look at his motion. The wrists. I don't expect many of you to master this technique, but I want you, Flynn; you, O'Brien; and you, Lovegrove to learn how to do this. Dean, I know you will want to, but you will not ever be passing a ball. Is this clear?'

I demonstrated it.

'It's no different to a torpedo punt,' Brother Hugh said. 'Same principle. It's a spiral. And we have Slaven's mother to thank for this.'

No one else mastered it that season, but we scored quite a few tries with cut-out passes. I had a good relationship with O'Brien, who played in the centres. He knew where to be before I threw the pass, and other times, I'd see the hole, throw it at the hole and he'd be there. It had won us the grand final the year before against Lithgow High and they had two blokes who were seventeen in their team. Illegal. But that's Publics. It just hardened our resentment of them. And made the win that much sweeter.

Generally speaking, Rugby League was compulsory and was taken very seriously by the Brothers. There were a few in the class who didn't play – Neville because of his eyesight, Thorley because of chalky bones, and Doyle, who had suffered a spontaneous pneumothorax and collapsed one lunchtime playing touch footy. His mother had written to Brother Hugh, and despite his willingness to play, he was deemed unable. Sometimes he'd sneak onto the field and play in our house competition on sports days, where he distinguished himself by proudly proclaiming he'd never once got his shorts dirty.

Sometimes Mum would come to the weekend football where she would occasionally encounter Brother Hugh.

Brother Hugh could not handle women at all. He went weirdo. He would almost convulse and struggle to speak. He made guttural noises. A sort of 'ggrrrnnngg'.

'Hello, Mrs Slaven, gggrrrnnnngg. Grrnnggg. Grrrnnnggg.' And his face would turn as red as beetroot from a can.

'Gnnrrgg, the passgnnrr, spiral, gnnnhhrrrr.'

'Oh. You like the torpedo pass, Brother? Good. It can have a deadly accuracy.'

'Grrnnngggg,' Brother Hugh responded, with desperate nodding.

Mum stared at him for a moment. I think she was worried he was having a heart attack or a stroke.

'Well, it's a beautiful day for football, Brother, not windy at all.'

'Grrnnngg, no, gnnnrrnngg, not gnnrrgg wind, no, no, gnnnrrrgg.'

Then Mum would hold him in her gaze and the noises he made would go on until she relieved him by moving on.

'Anyway, Brother, I'll leave you to it.'

He'd bow his head and almost explode with awkward discomfort.

'Yes, Mrs, gnnrrgh, Slaven gnnrrgh.'

Then Mum would whisper to me. 'He's mad, Roy. Certifiable. He's got to be.'

'He's okay when there aren't women about, Mum. Different bloke then.'

'I'll take your word for that.'

As I said, Mum didn't always come to the football. She said she didn't much like the crowd. A lot of the Publics would shout out things designed to put you off. And sometimes they initiated arguments, usually when a decision went against them. And sometimes the arguments would get really heated. And sometimes they ended in fights. A fight broke out beside Mum at one game and she said she had trouble 'biting her tongue'. She didn't much like seeing me get tackled either.

Chapter Three

'Prayer. Prayer is the only shield against Lucifer.'
FATHER JIM KEOGH, PARISH PRIEST

'Remember, boys, the blonder they are; the
dumber they are. Sit down, Marilyn.'
BROTHER HUGH CORCORAN

The summer Dad left was dry and hot. Not much to do until the cricket restarted. I spent a lot of time at the pool. It was fairly new. There was a toddlers' pool with a fountain and an Olympic pool. It was set on a slope. Wide concrete paths bordered a lush lawn bordered by a few trees and a ten-feet high wire mesh fence. The concrete was tessellated – light and dark. We'd lay on the light when it was hot and the dark when it was cool. There was a regular pool gang. Flynn was always there, O'Brien, Brewer, Brennan, Dean, Doyle and sometimes Doug Christian. Doug Christian was a Public who lived in Brewer's street near the tennis courts. None of us liked Doug Christian much. He would swear in front of the girls.

Dean and Doyle were interested in lifesaving. And lifesaving courses. Weird. They would time themselves doing laps of freestyle, breaststroke, sidestroke and water sculling. They were planning to do the Bronze Medallion. Most of the time we filled our days by diving in and bobbing about, doing exotic dives and bombing people. Any girl was fair game. And we'd swim underwater. Dean and Doyle could do a lap and a half underwater in one breath. I trained myself to do two laps underwater, a feat that's never been equalled. Brother Connor was there to witness it. He was astonished. 'Most impressive, Slaven. A skill that could be used somewhere, I suppose. Attaching mines to enemy vessels, perhaps.' The Vietnam War was underway.

We'd lie on the concrete in our togs and chat. We all wore Speedos. The pool manager, Mr Mulcahey, put speakers in the pool shop by the entrance and the radio would be broadcast across the whole area. 2LT or 2UW were the stations to listen to. Mainly it was deadshit music, but there were windows where the most popular songs of the day were played. We liked The Beatles a lot. Flynn didn't mind The Beach Boys; and Brewer, The Rolling Stones. We agreed that anyone who liked The Bachelors was a total dick.

●

Brother Connor liked The Bachelors. It was not uncommon for him to sing their hit 'I Believe' to himself when on playground duty. He raised the song in class.

'Hands up those who have heard the song "I Believe".'

Most hands went up.

'Hands down. Hands up those who have listened to the lyrics.'

Just as many hands go up.

'Hands down. Hands up those who, like me, love the song.'

Not a hand goes up. Brother Connor surveyed the room. He was annoyed.

'I don't believe you. I believe you love the song. All of you do. It's almost perfect. Lyrically. It's wholesome music, boys. Unlike much of the sick noise we hear on the radio these days.'

Back to the window sash.

'"I Believe". It's a song of hope, boys. Isn't it? It's beautiful. But. Is there something missing from our fine Bachelors' lyrics? Anyone? Slaven?'

'There's no mention of Rugby League, Brother.'

'No. There's not. I'll grant you that. Dean?'

'They don't mention Our Lord, Brother.'

'Well observed, Dean. Although, isn't God tacit to the song? Tacit? Doyle?'

'Does that mean implied, Brother?'

'Implied, yes. God in nature, boys. There is God in nature.' Brother Connor noticed Brewer scribbling. 'Read it out, Brewer, whatever it is you are writing. Come on. Share it with us.' Brewer started giggling. 'Read it out.'

'Umm . . . Every time I smell a silent Benson fart, a forest dies.'

Laughter. To Brewer's relief, even Brother Connor laughed. 'Ah, the barren poesy of the Tundra.'

•

Anyway, we'd meet at the pool, and the talk would generally start with whatever had been watched on television the night before. We didn't have television, but Dean did, Doyle did and Brewer did. They were keen on a show called *Peyton Place* and were totally besotted with a girl called Betty Anderson, a leading character. Doyle thought she was without doubt a Public. Dean agreed. She seemed to have no morals at all.

I was dead keen to see *Peyton Place* and went around to Brewer's one Thursday night to watch it. I had to sit on the floor, which was fine. They had a new twenty-one inch HMV and a forty-foot antenna, which meant they got Channel Nine and the ABC. The lower the house in the valley, the higher the antenna needed to be. Some needed to be sixty feet.

The whole family gathered in the lounge room with Mrs Brewer, Mr Brewer and Brewer's older sister, Yvonne, on the three-seater, and Brewer in a chair. It was a night Father Keogh dropped in – he was a regular on Thursday nights, apparently, which is why I was on the floor between Brewer's feet. Father Keogh sat in the other chair, which was the closest to the set.

It was fantastic watching television. I loved it all. The ads were great and Betty Anderson was exceptional. She was a spellbinding rhapsody of irresistible temptation. At the end of the show, Mr Brewer turned the television off and Father Keogh said it was the most un-Christian show he had ever seen and remonstrated with Mr and Mrs Brewer over them allowing Brewer and me, and especially Yvonne, to watch such a shameful, sinful programme. They were chastened, although Mr Brewer gave me a wink as Father Keogh spluttered and fiddled with his face with the sodden handkerchief.

I rode home. The house was dark because Mum wasn't back from Berlei's. Normally she'd be home just after half past twelve.

What a woman. Betty Anderson. Why Rodney Harrington would be interested in Allison MacKenzie was the flaw in the plot, because Betty Anderson had it all. All at the pool agreed with me. I wasn't telling them anything new. But raising the issue of Betty Anderson always garnered enthusiastic talk. Flynn said he thought Allison MacKenzie, Betty Anderson's rival for Rodney's affection, had a head like a busted cabbage. It was around that time that Brewer made the observation that he was waking up with a fat every morning. We all were. Dean thought it was because we'd seen Betty Anderson.

O'Brien said he'd never seen Betty Anderson and he woke with a fat as well. O'Brien said his problem was that he'd wake with a fat and need to go to the toilet for a wee. He said he had to mimic the walk of a chimpanzee to disguise his member as he moved from the bedroom, through the kitchen, and out the back to the dunny at the bottom of the yard.

Flynn said it's best to get rid of a fat before you wee and that weeing with a fat would give you cancer of the dick. This was very sobering information. None of us wanted dick cancer.

Dean said the best way to get rid of a fat was to hit it with a very cold spoon. His mum was a nurse. He reckons he'd seen his mum hit his dad's fat with a cold spoon. None of us believed that.

Brewer said he'd rather whack off. He said it worked out pretty well, because *Peyton Place* was on Thursday night and he'd have a good old whack Friday morning, thinking about Betty Anderson, and be able to get to confession on Friday night. He was only in mortal sin for about ten and a half hours.

Father Keogh gave a pretty passionate sermon about *Peyton Place* at Sunday mass. He tied it in with vital mission work going on in New Guinea and how important it was to donate to the church for this crucial work to continue. While New Guinea was important, he kept returning to *Peyton Place* and warned everyone to stop watching it. It didn't stop him dropping in on the Brewers on Thursday nights, though. Like clockwork. I started watching it at Dean's place, because Father Keogh wouldn't shut up over at Brewer's.

'What did she say, Mrs Brewer? She whispers all the time, this one.' Then, 'For the love of God, can you turn it up a little now?' 'Oh, she's a piece of work, that one. A wicked spalpeen. A floozy of the first order.' 'Oh, she's the very divil, that one. The divil incarnate.'

It was much quieter at Dean's. A bit of tut-tutting from Mrs Dean, the nurse, who didn't for a minute believe we had to watch it for homework.

Dean was very bright. And sensible. And dependable. He was big-boned and tall and fearless when running the Rugby League ball up into the defensive line. He was the only one among us the Brothers treated like an adult. He was born an adult. Dean had never received the strap. Not once.

•

While Mum was doing the shiftwork, I was able to see films at the Theatre Royal. No one ever checked our ages and I teamed up with Lyndon Lawless from Fourth Form who lived not too far away and we got to see *The Amorous Adventures of Moll Flanders*. We agreed that Kim Novak was as impressive as Betty Anderson. And, without a shadow of doubt, a Public. Brewer went to see it with Marsland, and they both agreed with me.

•

English class, as I said, was with Brother Hubert and would usually start with him reciting a poem from *Around The Boree Log* by John O'Brien. 'Said Hanrahan' was a favourite. Sometimes homework would be learning a stanza from an O'Brien poem by rote and one time he read us 'The Man From Snowy River', and we all thought it fantastic. He loved his bush poetry, did Sherb. He loved the bush.

Lithgow was experiencing the hottest summer anyone could remember and in mid-February Sherb took us outside, armed each of us with a box of matches and told us to burn off the blackberry bushes that were out of control near the oval on the eastern side of the school. After twenty minutes or so, a number of Littleton homes were under serious threat and the fire brigade was called. This happened quite a few times. Sherb had a poor reputation in that part of Littleton.

Sometimes Sherb would teach through the window. He'd stand in the garden bed and have a smoke. Sometimes he'd bot a smoke from Benson.

And sometimes he'd lose control. One day he completely lost it.

It was a windy Friday, second last period. A double English. Sherb had been struggling. He was tired of reading, tired of talking, tired of teaching and tired of us. Brennan was chasing Brewer around the perimeter of the room. Dean and Doyle had finished their Maths homework, their Science homework, their Geography assignment and were talking about where they might go looking for fossils on the weekend. Flynn got involved and said he'd go too. I was playing boxes with Marsland. Mahon had brought out his Alpine cigarettes and Benson was keen to try a menthol. They lit up. Benson thought it was 'shit'. It was noisy. Voices were raised because to be heard you had to shout. Everyone was shouting.

Sherb was over shouting. Sherb was over everything. He left the room.

We all carried on. Brennan and Brewer were back at their desks, exhausted and laughing. The fossil club had a weekend agenda and all was good.

After twenty minutes, Sherb entered the classroom at pace and began swinging a four-foot length of rubber with both hands like a broadsword, delivering fearful blows across our backs, heads, legs, arms – it was indiscriminate.

On this first occasion of what Doyle would later call 'Das Mayhem', he raised the rubber to strike O'Brien, who had the presence of mind to desperately say, 'I said a Hail Mary for you this morning, Brother.' This stopped him in his tracks. He nodded politely and moved on.

Ten wild swings of the rubber later, Marsland was in the crosshairs. Marsland was a large genial fellow blessed with a permanent smile. 'I said a Hail Mary for you this morning, Brother.'

Sherb propped and said, 'Marsland, I couldn't give a bugger.' Then proceeded to give his back a tremendous blow that sent him to the floor in agony.

After fifty or so violent swings of the rubber log, Sherb slumped with exhaustion. He breathed heavily.

There was a silence punctuated by currawongs and the groans of boys. I got a graze across the top of my head. I was fine. Dean was okay. Doyle had hidden under a desk. He was okay. Brennan was bleeding above the right eye from where his head had hit the sharp edge of the timber desk. Brewer had a bleeding gash to the back of his head where the framed picture of Saint John Baptist de La Salle had struck him when it fell off the wall. His head saved the glass from smashing. The Temperate Zone was the worst affected. Mills was in tears because his new set-square had been snapped. And his glasses were broken. Mitchell had been struck for the first time in his life. I saw it closely. He was hit clean across the side of the neck, which was now very red and swelling. His ears would be ringing. He was in tears. Mahon thought his arm might be broken. It wasn't.

Sherb stood up straight and looked about. He still breathed heavily. He shouldered the rubber club. He was to lug this thing about with him from that day until his health became an issue. He had fetched an axe and hacked off a huge thick length of stiff rubber matting from the floor of the Brothers' quarters to make it. Brewer and Benson started placing exercise books under their shirts before English from that day forward.

Benson lit up a Country Life. Sherb botted one, then placed the club along the chalk shelf under the blackboard, wiped the snot from his nose and rested against the front desk, which was askew. He was exhausted. He pulled a matchbox from his pocket and lit up. Dean collected the scattered lumps of coal from the floor and righted the scuttle.

Eventually, Sherb hurled his butt into the fireplace and his breathing returned to normal. He looked about the room, then at us carefully. 'God almighty, boys. Get off the floor. Sit up properly. Brewer, hang that picture back up where it belongs. Everyone else, sit up and fold your arms.'

He picked up the rubber log and walked the aisle, dragging it behind him. The Temperates were shaking with fear. 'I saw Esau sitting on a seesaw. Trochee's feet are short and long.'

•

Dean and Doyle were congratulated at assembly for being the first boys at the school to be qualified lifesavers. They'd successfully completed the Bronze Medallion, which meant they had swum the distances in the required time and learnt the techniques of rescue and recovery. They bored us all with talk of the Silvester–Brosch method of resuscitation. And they wore a small black-and-white official lifesaving patch on their swimmers. They must have thought it looked 'cool'. It didn't. It made them look like crawlers and dicks. They were already planning to upgrade to the Bronze Cross, which would mean another patch on the Speedos.

I never saw them actually rescue anyone.

Chapter Four

'Young people need the light of watchful guides
to lead them on the path of salvation.'
SAINT JOHN BAPTIST

'I much prefer a small man with a big heart
to a large man with a small heart.'
BROTHER HUGH CORCORAN

As Catholics, we had a long weekend coming up. Saint Joseph's Day was a holy day of obligation and, because it fell on a Sunday, the holiday was moved to the Monday. Word got out that Sherb was having a bushwalk. I liked walking with Sherb, many of us did. So after morning mass, with a sermon about what a top bloke Saint Joseph was, we gathered at the school and at about ten o'clock, Sherb emerged in civvies with his large straw hat and we set off.

Sherb might have been getting senile or it might have been something else, I don't know, but his behaviour was becoming more eccentric. Living in the Brothers' house must have been a challenge for anyone. It was cold and poorly appointed. What they got up to in their spare time, I haven't a clue. There was no television and they were wary of the radio. And Sherb had been there for a thousand years.

On this walk was me, Flynn, O'Brien, Dean, Doyle and Brewer. No representatives from the Temperate Zone. For an ancient man, Sherb set a cracking pace. He was well over six feet tall with a long stride. Our ambition was to get to Magpie Hollow, about four miles away. It was sunny and warm and windless.

We pretty much stuck to the road until Sherb decided it was time to go cross-country. We each picked up fallen boughs and fashioned them into quarterstaffs. Sherb liked to point out features like rock types, mainly sandstone and some granite, and Flynn picked up a rock Sherb said was porphyritic schist. Dean thought it was gneiss. Doyle was certain it was volcanic. I didn't really care one way or the other. Nor did O'Brien or Brewer.

Every now and then he'd stop and listen. 'What can we hear, boys?' We'd all stop. Silence. 'Shhh, boys. Hear that?' None of us could. 'There are honeyeaters about, boys. The Regent honeyeater. Eyes peeled.' And we'd move on. Other times he'd point out some of the trees. 'Look, boys, white box, yellow box and a red gum. All together. What a picture that would make. Imagine what Tom Roberts or Sir Arthur Streeton would do with that.' He then made it clear he was no fan of modern art.

'Art reached its highpoint with the Impressionists, boys. After that is nothing but confusion and madness.'

We saw magpies, kookaburras, choughs, king parrots, rosellas, cockatoos and a huge wedge-tailed eagle gorging on the carcass of a wombat. 'Nature, boys. Tooth and claw. Tooth and claw.'

Flynn and Doyle got to discussing whether Saint Joseph had been cuckolded or not. Flynn thought it arguable. Dean joined in with the view that Our Lady had not been unfaithful. Doyle agreed and added that it must have been hard for Saint Joseph, because people would have talked. 'There would have been gossip. He's not the real father, you know? That sort of thing.' Flynn agreed. 'He could have got into a lot of fights.'

At one point in the mid-afternoon, we were lazing about having a break, lying on our backs looking at the gathering clouds. Sherb was standing very still not twenty feet from us having a smoke. A large brown goanna emerged at pace from the tall grass and shimmied up Sherb's back, rested on his head and looked about. We were utterly stunned. Astonished. So was Sherb. He froze. The goanna had his front legs wrapped around Sherb's forehead. The tableau remained for what seemed minutes. We remained spellbound. Then Sherb started to twitch and the goanna leapt from his head and disappeared at a rate of knots.

Dean stood first. 'Are you all right, Brother?'

'Never felt closer to nature, Dean. Saint Joseph is looking over me today.'

We made our way down to the Coxs River and drank some water. No one had brought anything to eat or drink so the river water came as a welcome and necessary pleasure. We sat together by a bank and watched and listened with Sherb. Doyle and Dean seemed a bit worried about him. As far as I was concerned, he was just being Sherb.

'Still, boys,' he whispered. 'Stay very still.' He then pointed to the embankment on the opposite side of the river where, just beneath the surface, a platypus was swimming vigorously in a circle, occasionally breaking the water. Then there were two.

'Boys. Some things are beyond our comprehension and deliberately so. The platypus is one. It's one of these things. This is God playing with us. Our confusion must give him pleasure. We can offer up our confusion as confirmation of his greatness. It's pointless embarking on understanding. There is no understanding, boys. That path leads to madness.'

At that point, at that time, none of us could disagree with any of that.

Very quickly, the bucolic wonder of the moment was broken by a huge crack of lightning, followed instantly by thunder and then a downpour of terrible ferocity. We were all drenched in seconds.

Then it was a case of save yourself. Sherb headed up the slope with Dean, Doyle and Brewer in tow. Flynn said he knew a shortcut back to the school where our bikes were and it was he, O'Brien and me who struck out on a different course.

It was hard going. The rain was relentless and now driven by a pitiless wind. We walked for ages and it was starting to get quite dark. Flynn said he was hungry. O'Brien said he was cold. I was both. Eventually we clambered through a wire fence and came to a bitumen road. Flynn immediately started to put his thumb out to any car or truck that passed us by. It was too dangerous to walk on the shoulder of the road. We were ignored by two coal trucks, a Ford Anglia, a Morris Minor and a Hillman Minx. A Ford Falcon slowed down, looked promising, the windows were wound down and two Slater brothers shouted obscenities at us.

The Slaters were Publics. They loved fighting Catholics. Had we been twelve months older, they would have punched our heads in. Slaters hated Catholics. They hunted in packs. They used iron bars. They were serious.

We just stood there.

'You're a cunt and you're a cunt and you're a cunt. What the fuck are you looking at, cunt?'

We froze. We were relieved when we heard the engine rev up as they rounded the corner and sped off.

Mercifully, ten minutes later, a yellow Finley's Furniture delivery Holden utility stopped and the three of us tumbled into the cabin. It was a tight fit. Flynn sat on my lap. The driver was a friendly young fellow, with shocking acne, who liked to punctuate his speech with swearing. 'Where the fuck have you blokes been?' We explained the walking adventure and he thought we were 'out of your fucking minds'. He was happy he'd beaten the rain. He'd delivered a roll of Axminster carpet to a house in Hartley. The layers would be doing the job tomorrow morning. We knew, because he was working on a holy day of obligation, that he was a Public. We agreed later, though, that he was a decent bloke.

He was happy to drop us off at the school. I noticed Dean, Doyle and Brewer's bikes were still there so we knocked on the door of the Brothers' house. Brother Connor answered. He was eating a piece of heavily buttered toast and looked odd in his civvies. He wore a blue shirt, grey slacks and a purple jumper. We explained what had happened and he looked heavenward and called out behind him, 'Bertie's lost again.' Sherb was apparently Bertie in the house.

Brother Connor put on a raincoat and picked up the car keys from the console table upon which the new telephone sat. He was very business-like. 'O'Brien, Flynn, get home. Slaven, you're coming with me.'

In the car I shivered and fiddled with the heater. It annoyed Brother Connor a bit, because the white Valiant station wagon was brand new. 'Don't you break anything there, Slaven.'

'Try not to, Brother.'

After a short while the heat really kicked in and I started to be able to concentrate. I told him Magpie Hollow was the starting point. We turned right at Gould's Hill and about a mile down the road saw the group of four. Sherb was being held closely by Dean and Doyle. They were clearly on their last legs. Sherb appeared to have lost a shoe. It was getting really dark. We stopped and they climbed into the back seat. Brother Hubert was freezing, his straw hat now an eccentric shape. Dean had torn his trousers climbing over a barbed wire fence and Brewer just shook. Doyle looked relieved.

'I'm missing a shoe,' said Sherb. Doyle, who had clambered into the rear of the station wagon, said he had it and passed it over to Sherb, who cradled it in his lap.

All in all, it was a typical Sherb adventure. Nothing else was said on the way back to the school. Brother Connor sang 'I Believe' quietly to himself.

The house was empty when I got home in the dark. At least the rain had stopped. I had a long hot bath and found some fish fingers in the fridge freezer. I fried them and they came up pretty good with tomato sauce. Then I lit the fire for Mum. It was just the beginning of Autumn, but it was cold. Mum hated the cold.

•

I played junior cricket in the mornings on Saturday and senior in the afternoons. I can never remember being given out in junior cricket. It must have happened, but there is no record. Usually the umpires, like Mr Hammond or Mr Bannerman, would talk to one of the Brothers and I would be asked to retire and let someone else have a bat. I remember getting a century in the final against PBC Royals in the under twelves. One hundred and five, not out. The *Lithgow Mercury* newspaper sent a photographer to our house and Dad got into a fight with him. The photograph was never taken.

Junior cricket had four teams: La Salle, Wallerawang, PBC Royals and PBC Regals. Both Police Boys Club teams were Publics, as was most of Wallerawang. Regals were easybeats – whoever organised the Police Boys stacked all the good players into the Royals. It was a totally corrupt system.

Regals had one decent player, Greg Pitt, who could bat and bowl a bit and even seemed a very decent fellow. Smiled a lot. Wanted to engage. But he was a Public, so we kept things pretty formal.

The Royals had a good batsman in Jimmy Bannerman and a good bowler in Ronnie Horner. Both, like me and Doyle, played seniors in the afternoon. Our seniors had a couple of the Brothers in the team. Brother Hugh and Brother Michael. Harold, our Geography teacher, was the captain and Brother Hugh would get under his skin by asking for a bowl at the end of each over.

'My bowl, Harold, is it?'

'Not yet, Brother.'

In the juniors I opened the batting with Doyle. He should never have been an opener because he didn't handle fast bowling well at all. Fear and panic made him stupidly aggressive.

'Just have a look at it,' I'd say to him. 'Let a few go.'

But he wouldn't. In all the years we opened together – under twelves, under fourteens and now under sixteens – we had a partnership of over fifty only once.

Watsford Oval. La Salle versus PBC Royals. Under sixteens. November 1966. Doyle was captain, because he was a crawler. He'd been captain for three years. Every Saturday he would arrive with a plan in the back pocket of his shorts. The plan was nothing but field placings and names. He would read it out to us. 'Roy, first slip.' The plan was the same every week. Every year.

He could bowl a bit. Medium pace, leg cutters mainly. He could really control his length. He could never get me out, but I found it hard to score against him whenever we trained together in the nets. Which was often.

He always opened the batting because no one else wanted to. They were scared of Ronnie Horner's speed. Doyle won the toss and we batted. I took strike and blocked two balls from Horner and let the rest go. He was genuinely quick.

Change of ends and Jimmy Bannerman says, 'Boys, let's welcome the De La Salle captain.' And the team gives a polite clap. We did the same when Bannerman came in to bat. Doyle would say, 'Blokes, let's welcome the PBC Royals captain.' Polite applause. It was a tradition. A Public one, probably.

Hallinan bowls to Doyle. Medium pace. It's short, I would have hooked it, but Doyle walks into it, gets cramped and spoons it without control over the slips for four. He was lucky he wasn't out first ball.

I'd have put a fly slip in, but Bannerman doesn't.

Hallinan's next ball is short on the leg side, Doyle moves inside it and it clips the top of his bat handle and sails into the fence behind the wicketkeeper. Then he winks at me. I just shrug, I have nothing to say. This is mad batting.

Then two elaborate drives that missed the ball. One was really close. Jimmy Bannerman, at first slip, appealed and I was surprised when Mr Bannerman, the umpire and his father, shook his head and broadcast, 'Nout even close, son.' I think that's what he said, because he had a thick Scottish brogue that could cut steel. It was a foreign language.

Then a defensive shot off the middle of the bat got Doyle three, and I finished off the over with a nice drop and run, which with an overthrow turned into two.

Two overs and we're none for thirteen. Then it's Horner to Doyle. Doyle is walking down the pitch as Horner delivers a quick ball on a good length on the off stump. He attempts to drive it, catches a thick outside edge and it's gone to blazes over deep third man for six. A fluke.

It took a few minutes to regather the ball. I got talking to Mr Bannerman. Couldn't understand a word. I think he was complaining about the quality of the mats or something. Dunno. I just nodded. Agreed with every noise he made.

Horner drops the next one short and it nearly takes Doyle's head off. He picks it up late. Shakes him up, too, I reckon. Two more wild swings and misses. Then he repeats the thick outside edge with the identical result to the first. Six.

Then he's hit twice in successive deliveries. Both in the same place, on the inside of his right leg, just below the box. He's wearing shorts and there is no protection. Both balls had jagged in off a tear in the mat and become fast off-breaks. Must have hurt like fuck. I walk down to check on him, because he's doubled over and rubbing his leg.

Ronnie Horner comes down to him as well. 'You okay?' There was no malice in Ronnie Horner, he seemed a lovely bloke. Grinned a lot. But, a Public.

Doyle said he's fine and mans up. Half the top of his right leg is going black. Horner drops another one short, Doyle swipes and skies it. We run. 'Three,' he says to me as we cross. Wayne Hammond drops the ball on the leg fence. We run three comfortably.

Hallinan puts down a ball to Doyle that would have been called a wide but for Doyle playing a cut shot. Again, the ball catches the top edge and it's another six. We're none for thirty-three and I've scored two runs. The next ball is short and he awkwardly parries it away and we run two. He charges the next ball and skies it straight over the head of Hallinan where it's again dropped. Another two. Then Doyle takes one on the left arm. It hurts, but it'll pass. A stinging graze. Wasn't flush. Two wides followed. Then a couple of blocks.

By the time Doyle nicked one from Horner to the wicket-keeper we were fifty-three runs. Doyle had scored forty-seven of them. But it didn't happen often. Usually I was left not out on sixty or so in a total score of seventy-five. Doyle was lucky if he managed ten runs. This day he was sore but happy.

•

In the men's A-grade cricket I was on a bit of a roll. I had been seeing the ball really well and opened the innings each week with Harold, and often had to retire to give someone else a bat. In the last seven matches I hadn't been dismissed and had an average of five hundred and seven. Some teams thought it unfair and wanted me to play in Sydney. But it wasn't feasible. I didn't want to. And Mum couldn't afford the train fare.

A weird story. This happened last year. One lunchtime, back at school. Brother Hugh called me over to him. He was under a pine tree. He was very serious and spoke very quietly. He said, 'You're batting well.'

'Yes, Brother.'

'I want you to get out. Get yourself out. On Saturday. For twenty-one runs. It's public relations. Understood?'

I nodded but didn't understand at all. I told Mum when I got home. Mum told Dad and he hit the roof. He took me up to the school and we confronted Brother Hugh. After a few minutes, I was told to wait in the car and Dad and Brother Hugh kept talking.

When Dad got back in the car and we were driving home, he said to me, 'Twenty-one runs. On Saturday. Retire hurt. Or something.'

I began to speak.

'It's for the parish,' he said. Whatever that meant.

It gave me the shits. But I retired hurt. On twenty-one runs. Said I felt sick. And I did. Apparently it was to do with Harold taking bets with a local bookie on the outcomes of games. I suppose he needed the money to pay for the packages that arrived from Sydney. I tried to get to the bottom of it, but Dad said it was best not to know and to forget about it. I heard Mum arguing with Dad, but she quickly dropped it as well.

I was never asked to get out on a specific score again. But definitely something weird had gone on.

•

One Monday morning Brother Hugh called me into his office. I thought I was in trouble, but he said that Brian Booth was visiting the town and wanted to see me batting in the nets at the Glanmire. Brian Booth was a test cricketer who had captained Australia in two tests when Bobby Simpson was injured. I had listened to at least three Brian Booth innings on Brewer's radio, called by Alan McGilvray. Booth was in town giving a clinic to the A graders.

I was really excited. I told Doyle. He thought it was fantastic and asked me if he could come and watch. I said that'd be fine.

There was just me and Jimmy Bannerman waiting at the nets for Brian Booth to turn up. And he did, with a couple of other blokes in tracksuits who carried the kit. And another bloke in a grey suit. One of the blokes in a tracksuit was called Eddie and the other Mike. The bloke in the suit didn't have a name. Eddie and Mike were first-grade bowlers from Sydney.

Jimmy and I padded up. We were both fifteen. I went in first. Brian Booth stood outside the net behind me. He said he just wanted me to keep the ball out and asked Eddie and

Mike to send a few balls down. Eddie was quick. It took a while to get used to the speed. He clean bowled me twice in the first four balls. Brian said not to worry and to take guard on the middle stump rather than the leg. I did that. And then I started to really see the ball. The bowlers rotated and sent down about fifty balls at me and twice I straight drove them to buggery. No one got me out again in that session.

Doyle was watching from behind the bowlers.

Eventually, Mr Booth said, 'That's enough,' and I left the net for Jimmy Bannerman. Jimmy went okay but we had to stop when he took one on the glove. He was worried his finger might have been broken. It was pretty bruised. Mr Booth took me aside and asked me what I wanted to do with my career. I said I'd never really thought about it. He said he wanted to talk to my father. I told him where Dad probably was and suggested he talk to Mum. He said, 'God has given you the talent, young man. And there is no doubt in my mind that you will be playing for Australia before you turn twenty.'

Because of Mum's work commitments, Mr Booth couldn't talk to her. Eventually Mum was called up to the school and she spoke to Mr Booth on the telephone there, because we didn't have one at home. She said she was very proud of me.

The night after the net session with Mr Booth I lay in bed and dreamt of playing in a test match. I fell asleep and the dream continued. I dreamt that Doyle was at the other end, and I had to shepherd the strike. I'm on ninety-nine. We still needed five runs to win the match and Doyle was the last man in. We were in the second last over before stumps on the last day of the match. We could either win. Or draw. Or lose, if he got out.

It was a nightmare. He had to survive two balls from England's champion fast bowler John Snow for me to face the last over, get my hundred and win the match. Snow is fast. Very fast. And he's on a hat-trick. I can see the sheer terror in Doyle's eyes. So can John Snow. He smells blood. Doyle can hardly hold the bat, he is shaking so much.

The slips are openly laughing at him. 'Don't think this laddie can play,' says the second slip, with an accent just like Mr Bannerman's.

Third slip says, 'I've got a feeling Snowy might kill this laddie.'

'Hope they've got an ambulance ready.'

'They say you never get over it. Getting killed, like.'

The umpire holds up play. He's laughing so much he needs to wipe his eyes. Things settle. Snow moves in. Snow delivers. It's a swinging bullet on middle stump. Doyle didn't see it at all. Didn't look. Didn't try to look. He just stepped away and threw his bat wildly hoping for the best.

The ball finds the slightest piece of the back of Doyle's bat and sails over the head of Alan Knott, the wicketkeeper. Four runs. Ironic cheers from the crowd. It might be the MCG.

Doyle and I meet in the middle. We need one run. I need one run. They need one wicket. Doyle says, 'I've dreamt of this moment, Roy. I think I've got this bloke's measure. Look and learn.' And he winks at me. My heart sinks. I know he's going to get out. I feel like I am in his dream and have no control. Snow steams in. I can't look.

I wake suddenly in a sweat, with a feeling of frustration and urgency and having lost an important match. Or a good friend. I don't like it. And I'm wondering whether Dad is wearing my Kangaroo jersey or whether he's sold it. Or just lost it.

Chapter Five

'I don't want excuses. What use are
they to anyone? I want results.'
Brother Connor

'Boys, don't imagine there is any man capable of fully
understanding the mind of God. Or understanding
life. We take the leap of faith, boys. Faith is all.'
Brother Hugh Corcoran

Back at the pool. The grassy area on the slope by the deep
end was considered the Catholic area. The flat grass on
the other side of the deep end was the Publics'. Barbara and
Deirdre and Margot and Carmel from Saint Pat's would often
join Flynn, O'Brien, Brennan, Brewer, Dean, Doyle and me.
They had good stories about the nuns and were a bit anxious as
to what was going to happen next year. The Wyndham Scheme
had been introduced and the Intermediate Certificate had been
replaced by the School Certificate, meaning an extra year at

school. The current Fourth Form was the first to do the new
School Certificate, but what was worrying the girls was that,
next year, Saint Pat's and De La Salle were to be combined.
The girls would be joining us at La Salle. We weren't worried
at all. We were looking forward to it. The girls, less so.

We wondered how the girls would get on with Brother
Connor, and more importantly the principal, Brother Hugh.
Brewer did a good impersonation of Brother Hugh and tried to
prepare the girls for what to expect. 'Barghrrnbara gnnnrrrgh
ghrrrrgh, gnhrrgh. GhhnnrrghDeirdre, ghhnnrrgh.'

Our girls wore modest one-piece swimming costumes.
Not so, the Publics. We'd often stare across the pool at the
bikini-clad girls with names like Vicki and Sharon and Julie.
Flynn had a good eye. He reckoned he could tell whether a
girl had had a root or not, just by her demeanour. I didn't have
that skill. I only had eyes for Susan Morgan. And she never
came to the pool.

I asked Barbara about it and she said Susan's parents wouldn't
let her. So for a while there, Susan Morgan and I communicated
through letters. I really liked Barbara and I trusted her to pass
on my letters, which she was more than happy to do. And she
would pass me Susan's replies. Her letters were glorious. The
paper was perfumed and had a coloured border. She dotted her
'i's' with tiny circles and signed off with 'xxx'. My letters to
her were usually about my cricket scores or what was going
on in the classroom with Brother Connor and Sherb, and hers
were about how strict her parents were and how she was having

trouble with Sister Pius and, disturbingly, the prospect of her moving to Mittagong if her dad got the position he was after with an accounting firm. This was very bleak news.

Whenever a girl walked past, we'd all look at Flynn and he'd either nod, meaning she'd had a root, or shake his head, meaning she hadn't. Flynn was worldly. He had older brothers and they had obviously given him a first-class apprenticeship in the ways of women. He was a student of women and took his studies very seriously.

Flynn was in love with Vicki Westwood, whom he said hadn't. And I could see why he loved her. She was funny. She got it. Whatever 'it' was. And she was a Public, which made her exotic. Vicki Westwood was a source of fascination for us all. She swore a bit. She said 'shit'. In fact, she spoke like we boys did. And she liked Rugby League and pies and cars. Her brother Wayne had a black Holden X2 so she knew what she was talking about. She wasn't pretty like Susan Morgan, but she had what Mum would call 'personality'. And she seemed to fit in with the Catholic girls, although Carmel thought she was 'cheap', whatever that meant. Maybe saying 'shit' made her cheap.

Flynn asked Vicki Westwood to the pictures to see *One Million Years BC* at the Theatre Royal and she said yes. They went one Friday night. Flynn said it was the best film he had ever seen and Raquel Welch was 'totally, totally Public'. He said he preferred her to Betty Anderson and that was saying something. Vicki Westwood liked it, too. And for a time there, we didn't see much of Flynn, and he and Vicki Westwood walked holding hands. Flynn had a real girlfriend. He said many of the Public girls were just like Vicki Westwood and he began to sit opposite us at the pool, with the Publics, and Dean thought he was probably in a state of mortal sin. Doyle thought it very possible. I wasn't sure. I couldn't see a real problem with it.

So we sat there, Dean, Doyle, Brewer, Brennan and me and Barbara and Deirdre and Carmel and Anne, and we watched Flynn. And Vicki Westwood. Normie Rowe's 'Ooh La La' blared out of the kiosk speakers. At one point, Flynn and Vicki Westwood kissed.

'Brazen,' said Carmel.

Brewer and Brennan applauded.

'Don't,' said Carmel, 'you're just encouraging them.'

Then Flynn looked across at us and gave a thumbs up. Vicki Westwood saw him do it, laughed and theatrically threw herself on him and they rolled together as one on the grass.

Doyle, just to annoy Carmel, said they made a beautiful young couple.

'Oh, please. Don't make me sick.'

Then Flynn and Vicki Westwood joined their towels together and lay in each other's arms.

'That's real love,' said Doyle.

'Don't be ridiculous,' said Carmel. 'Love isn't making a public exhibition of yourself.'

I think most of us boys would have traded places with Flynn in a heartbeat.

Ten minutes later, Doyle stands and asks if anyone is interested in wandering over to have a chat to Flynn. I stand. There are no other takers.

Carmel is incensed. 'You are going to look ridiculous.'

Deirdre and Barbara wish us luck.

We both leave our towels on the slope and head off around the deep end of the pool and enter Public territory. We are not heckled. We are ignored. Self-consciously, we stand over Flynn and Vicki Westwood. Vicki Westwood is talking to a friend called Janet. Flynn is sunbaking with his eyes closed. Vicki Westwood introduces us to Janet. 'These are friends of Jeff's. Roy and John. This is Janet.'

Flynn opens his eyes. 'What's going on?' he says.

Doyle says, 'We felt like a walk.'

Janet asks Doyle about the patch on his costume.

'It's a lifesaver's patch.'

'Are you a lifesaver?'

Doyle nods, sheepishly.

'So, if I'm drowning, what are you going to do?'

'Umm . . . Swim to you, grab your arm and twist you around and take hold of you and sidestroke you to the wall.'

I say, 'That's just for starters. Don't get him onto Silvester–Brosch.'

Janet says, 'I'd be happy just to be taken hold of and side-stroked to the wall. Any day of the week.' And she winks at Vicki Westwood and together they laugh.

Me and Doyle sit on the grass and look across to our group on the slope. They look an odd bunch. They are staring at us. Barbara waves. I wave back. Carmel says something and Dean nods sagely and Brewer and Brennan laugh.

Flynn tells Janet that I am destined to play cricket and football for Australia. Janet looks at me. 'Oh, is that you? You're Roy Slaven. My brother hates you.'

'Why?'

'He can never get you out. He's been trying for years.'

We stayed with Flynn and the Publics for about ten minutes before ambling back to our towels and our group. Janet was very chatty and funny. Just like Vicki Westwood.

Doyle says, 'What an interesting experience. Janet and Vicki Westwood enjoy smut as much as we do. But to them it's not sinful. Not sinful at all.'

I nodded. He was right.

Our group looked at us closely when we resettled.

Carmel says, 'Well? What did you talk about?'

Doyle says, 'Sin, Carmel. We talked about sin.'

'Well, you were in the right place.'

•

I got to see *One Million Years BC* with Lyndon Lawless a week later and I could see exactly what Flynn was talking about.

Raquel Welch had obviously been put on this earth to torment Catholic boys. I asked Sherb about it one day as he was having a smoke in the garden. He said that God put many traps before Catholic boys and described 'Miss Welch', as he called her, as a slut. He admitted, though, that he had never seen her, but if she 'was anything like Sophia Loren, she was without doubt a shameless slut. Avoid sluts, my boy, they will put you in the fast lane to eternal damnation.'

I didn't know Sophia Loren, but I was suddenly very interested. Flynn knew of her, as did Doyle, O'Brien and Dean. Brewer nicked a *Post* magazine from Stan Kuzmac, the barber, and showed me a picture of Sophia Loren in a bikini. She put Betty Anderson into fourth place behind Miss Novak and Miss Welch. No doubt the four of them provided a lot of material for the confessional.

Sometimes Father Keogh would turn up at the school to hear our confessions. He'd sit in the front room of the Brothers' quarters with the curtains drawn and the lights out and we'd take turns to leave the classroom. Benson said he was going to confess to having had a root. Brewer said he would, too. Together, they concocted a story. Benson was in there for a fair while. So was Brewer.

When I went in, Father Keogh was in a state of some agitation. His handkerchief was sodden. He dealt with me pretty quickly. I confessed to saying 'fuck' a few times, and 'shit' of course, and mentioned that girls were pretty much uppermost in my mind. He gave me a decade of the rosary and I polished that off pretty quickly while I had a cream bun from the tuckshop, and felt a lot lighter being in a state of grace.

Then a gust of wind blew the icing sugar from the top of the bun into my eye and onto my blazer. 'Shit!' I said. And in that thoughtless moment, the state of grace was gone. Confession was ten minutes ago and saying shit was a venial sin. If I died between now and the next confession, I'd have time in purgatory in agony waiting for someone like Benson or Brewer to say some Hail Marys on All Souls' Day to get me out. And it meant I wouldn't be going to communion on Sunday and everyone would know I was in a state of sin.

Brother Connor would sometimes take note of the boys he thought were most likely in sin.

'Slaven?'

'Yes, Brother?'

'Just out of interest, and for our amusement, could you describe, for us all, your vision of Hell?'

I stood. 'You burn, Brother. It's like a huge bonfire and you are forced to stand in the middle of it. And you are there forever.'

Brother Connor nodded. 'It could well be acid, you know. It may not be fire, strictly speaking. Acid would certainly be a painful experience. You could be dipped naked, holus-bolus, into a vast steaming vat of boiling acid, Slaven.'

Doyle put his hand up.

'Hand down, Doyle, I'm not finished.' He moved towards me. 'There would be torture, first.' He paused. Thorley was scared. So was Mills. The whole Temperate Zone was shit scared. 'The first thing the devil would do is tell you what he's going to do to you.' He paused for effect. '"I will tear each nail from your fingers and toes. With red-hot pliers. Then rip your teeth from your mouth. One by one. Then tear out your tongue. Then I will peel your skin off with a vegetable grater. Bamboo sticks will be plunged into your ears and your eyes removed by voracious pus-laden rats. Then you will be lowered into the vat of acid for all eternity." This, Lucifer would then do. And then you might think Lucifer would put his feet up and have a cup of tea. But no. No, boys. He would pull you out of the vat. And do it to you again.' He looked around at the sombre and fearful faces of his audience. He was well pleased. 'I wouldn't fancy being in sin. Wouldn't fancy it at all. On your feet, Benson. Name three types of triangles.'

Benson momentarily panicked and glanced at Doyle.

Anyway, after confession with Father Keogh at the school, I bumped into Benson and Brewer, who were behind the toilets having a smoke. They were cacking themselves. Benson said Father Keogh wanted him to go over his story in detail. 'I said she was a Public, Father. Kay. Kay something. A bit older than me and she forced me into it. It was behind the grandstand at the showground and she just took all her clothes off and said, "Give it to me, Benson." So I did.'

Brewer shared his version with me. 'Bless me, Father, for I have sinned. I had a root with Kay Green, Father. Couldn't help it, Father. I was walking home by the showground and she just appeared in front of me. She was in the nude, Father. "Come on, Brewer," she said, Father. "Come on, Brewer, I want you to give me a good hard root." I said, "But, Kay, I've got to get home for tea." "Root me first and then have your tea." So I did, Father. Twice.'

Chapter Six

'The young should be able to see in your
wisdom how they should behave.'
SAINT JOHN BAPTIST

'Gggggnnngh, MrsgnnnrrrrrrrSlaven, gnnnghgh.'
BROTHER HUGH CORCORAN

F ather Keogh must have suspended the law of confessional
confidentiality and said something to Brother Hugh,
because he called out Benson and Brewer at assembly that day
and gave each of them six. Then he told the assembly that at
all times we should respect the sacraments of the church and,
in particular, show respect to the priesthood. And the next day
Brother Connor gave us a sex education lesson.

He stood by the window, examining it, as usual. Then he
turned and said, 'Serious matter, boys. Procreation.'

He looked heavenward, searching for the right words. 'Boys,

you will be aware of an organ that sits beneath the waist. This is the penis and it must never be touched or played with.'

This got our attention. Benson started giggling. So did Brewer.

'Beneath the penis, boys, is a sack, a sacred sack, and this sack must never ever be touched. This sack houses seed, boys. Spermatozoa.' With chalk he drew a pretty poor penis and testicles on the blackboard. 'The spermatozoa swims from the sacred sack up into the penis and beyond. Each seed is potentially a baby, boys. Each seed is, therefore, sacred. To abuse yourself is to murder unborn babies and is a mortal sin. But sex is not to be feared. It's just like . . . just like sneezing.'

Benson sneezed. We all laughed, the waddy came out and Benson got four.

•

Flynn said he'd seen Father Keogh walking around behind the grandstand at the showground. It might have been true, I don't know.

•

It wasn't much later that I happened to be riding past Susan Morgan's place. It was something I did pretty regularly on the off-chance she might be in the front yard. She never was. But this time a large Henry Dick removalists van was parked in the driveway and furniture was being loaded into it. Her dad must have taken the job at Mittagong.

I was nearly in tears. I had imagined us walking and holding hands, just like Flynn and Vicki Westwood. I had imagined introducing her to Mum and them getting on real well, and her coming to watch the cricket finals and then the football, and then next year she would have been with me in the same class at De La Salle and we could have sat near each other and I could have basked in her smile and warmth and friendship all day, every day until the day we married, and Dad would have turned up with Uncle Baz's jersey and all would have been forgiven, and the spermatozoa could have swum towards her in a perfect way, and God would have blessed us, and Father Keogh would have had his teeth fixed for the wedding, and Mr Booth would have come and told me I was opening the batting for Australia against England at the Sydney Cricket Ground, and Mum and the new Mrs Susan Slaven would have sat in the members' stand with Sir Donald Bradman and watched the match where I took guard on middle stump and batted flawlessly all day, scoring a double century in the final over before stumps of my maiden test.

•

Instead I just rode about town. As I rode down Sandford Avenue, I saw Doyle, who'd been bailed up by two Publics. I didn't know their names. I pulled up and got off the bike. There was a bit of pushing and shoving going on.

One of them turned to me. A big red-haired bloke. He said, 'What are you looking at, cunt?'

He'd got me at a really bad time. I didn't say anything, I just punched him as hard as I could in the stomach. He was winded and went down. The other bloke released Doyle, turned to me and I punched him in the face. A tooth broke. I nodded to Doyle, who seemed mightily relieved, and we walked off together, pushing our bikes. 'Who were they?' I asked.

'Penrose and Hiscock.'

'Which is which?'

'Hiscock's the bloodnut.'

'Fuck'n Publics.'

Doyle said he was going to the Railway Institute, near the co-op, and did I want to come. I was at a loose end.

We walked off the street into a dimly lit library. Lots of books behind glass. And an old bloke reading at a desk with a lamp. It was silent. Doyle said hello to the bloke and wrote his name and the date and time in a large blue register. Then we walked into another room. It was large. Doyle turned on the lights and there was a full-sized snooker table. Together we lifted the cream cotton cover to reveal the deep green baize.

There were about twenty cues in a rack against the wall, beside which was a brass score-counter. Some of the cues were at least eight feet long and had weird metal shapes attached to the ends. Doyle grabbed the triangle and racked the balls. 'Pick a cue, Roy.' I did.

I'd never played snooker before. I'd never been in a place like this before. For the mood I was in, it was perfect. Doyle's father worked at the railway so he was allowed to visit the institute. It was like being part of Lithgow's most exclusive club. A whole room, all this stuff, just to ourselves. Doyle showed me how to use the bridge and how to score and what the rules were. He said it was a place he could come to when things got a bit strange at home. I told him I felt like shit because Susan Morgan was leaving Lithgow.

'Where's she going?'

'Mittagong.'

'Where's that?'

'I dunno. South. South of Wollongong.'

'Is it near Austinmer? Dad's from Austinmer.'

'Where's that?'

'Near Wollongong.'

'It's probably near, then. How does that help?'

'It doesn't.'

I broke and a red went into a pocket. Then, on Doyle's advice, I lined up the black. Took my time. It went in.

'Nice shot,' said Doyle.

Then I took another red. I had never played snooker before. But I got it. We'd played bobs once at Uncle Baz's place and I'd had a game of billiards on a shit table at Mount Lambie once with Dad. But this surface was perfect. I could put the ball wherever I wanted to.

Doyle said, 'You're Minnesota Fats, Roy.'

Then I sank a pink, a red, a black, a red, a blue, a red, a pink again, then the red and the black. Then red, black, red, black. And red, yellow, green, brown, blue, pink, black . . . game over.

'I'm never going to see her again.'

Doyle then sings the chorus of 'You're Going to Lose That Girl'. It's a Beatles song I like. I sing with him. At the end we nod at each other.

'I kissed her once. Just once. After mass, behind the sacristy. I was waiting around outside hoping she might appear. She did. She wanted to check my nose; the break had healed well. She held my head in her hands. We looked into each other's eyes. And it just happened. It was . . . nature. Angels sang. It was "Here, There and Everywhere". And her arms reached around me and mine around her and time was . . . there was none. I wanted every bit of her and she wanted me. I could feel it. It had a taste, Doyle, a flavour, a texture.'

I was exaggerating the story to impress Doyle. The truth was that our lips had merely brushed, but it was the intense electricity of the moment that I was trying to convey. I think Doyle knew this by the way he looked at me.

He then said, 'It's better to have loved and lost than never to have loved at all.'

I said I liked that.

'Tennyson,' said Doyle, 'Brother Michael's favourite.'

Doyle gets the triangle and racks the balls. 'Paul is melody and John is soul.'

I loved talking about the Beatles. 'Yeah. But George adds something.'

Doyle nodded. 'He does. Something. Definitely. Did you see *Help!*?'

'Yeah.'

'I went with my aunty and she found George the sexiest.'
It was the first time I had heard the word 'sexiest'.

He went on. 'I've ordered *Sergeant Pepper.* Should be in soon.
Come over some time. House to myself Saturday nights.'

He broke. Nothing went in. I racked up seventy points.
Doyle said he would manage me, if I wanted him to. He said
we could make a fortune. There were prizes to be won. In
the clubs. He'd worked in the clubs. I said I'd think about it.

I liked the Railway Institute. I liked the snooker. And I liked
Doyle, crawler that he was. He made sure everything was put
back in its place before he turned the light off.

We pushed our bikes down Main Street. A carload of Slaters
drove by in a hotted-up Falcon XR. They shouted something
and whistled at two Public girls standing outside the Bluebird
Café. They were wearing miniskirts. The car stopped, holding
up traffic, and the girls stood close to the car and words were
exchanged. Someone blew their horn and a Slater climbed out
of the back seat and shouted, 'Fuck'n do that again. I dare ya.'
Then they revved loudly, the offended Slater hopped back in
and the Falcon laid a bit of rubber as they took off. The girls
laughed.

We said together, 'I'd never buy a Falcon.' We laughed at
the synchrony. Then we rode home our separate ways.

Chapter Seven

'We're more popular than Jesus now. I don't know
which will go first, rock and roll or Christianity.'
JOHN LENNON

'Example makes a much greater impression than words.'
SAINT JOHN BAPTIST

Sundays after mass I'd sometimes go over to Brewer's to
watch world championship wrestling. I thought it was
bullshit, but Brewer said it was real. To me, it was so obviously
fake. It was just a ballet. There was nothing I could say that
would dissuade Brewer from his belief that it was real though.

They had 'stars' from all over the world, such as Brute
Bernard and Spiros Arion and Killer Kowalski, and some
locals, like Larry O'Dea and Roy Heffernan. They were just
putting on a show. There were highly choreographed moves
like 'the flying mare' or the 'stepover toe hold'. Some bouts
were called 'scientific', which meant boring. Some had unique

deadly holds like 'the claw hold' or 'the sleeper hold' or 'the atomic drop'.

Mainly I went because Mrs Brewer made scones, and she'd bring in a plate each for Brewer and me with some jam and cream. It was the best food in the world. And usually she'd wrap a few in a brown paper bag for me to take home to Mum. Mrs Brewer was always asking how Mum was getting on and whether there had been any news of Dad. The response was pretty well always the same. 'Yeah, Mum's real well, thanks, Mrs Brewer.' And, 'No, we haven't heard anything from Dad. As far as we know, he's still in Caragabal.'

Mrs Brewer was concerned that she hadn't seen Mum at mass. All I could do was shrug. Mum was busy. Mum was earning money for two people. Mum had started making dresses for other people, mainly people she knew at Berlei's, or their friends.

Her Saturdays were taken up with women having fittings in our lounge room, which worked out well because I was out all day at cricket. It was good for Mum, because she was making friends. Kathy Wilson was one. Mum made her a few dresses and a costume she was wearing in a play she was doing with the Lithgow Theatre Group. It was called *Ass and Philosophers*. Mum said it was a 'period' dress. I didn't see the show, and nor did Mum because she was working, but Kathy Wilson encouraged Mum to get out a bit.

We talked about it. 'There's a group going to the RSL Club, Saturday night. They've asked me along.'

'Do you want to go, Mum?'

'Not much.'

She stood at the sink, staring out through the window at the coal heap. 'But it might get me a bit more dressmaking work. We need the money.'

'It's a dance, is it?'

'Yeah. And a meal, I think.'

'Who'll be there?'

'Kathy will pick me up. It'd be her theatre group friends, I think. Couple of teachers from the high school.'

'I think you should go then, Mum. I could go over to Doyle's, maybe. Listen to some records. He's asked me over.'

'I'll think about it,' she said.

I think she wanted to go but wondered about how it would look, a married woman out by herself.

•

Father Keogh had kept coming around. One time he came with another priest, Father Kane. Father Kane was much younger than Father Keogh, but his Irish accent was just as thick.

'Mrs Slaven, this is Father Kane.'

'Hello, Father Kane.'

Father Kane nodded and looked at his shoes.

'I'll suppose you'll both be looking for a cup of tea?'

'That would be marvellous, Mrs Slaven.' Father Kane looked at me. 'You're the footballing fellow?'

'I play a bit, Father, yes.'

'Would you be thinking about the Shamrocks, at all?'

Father Kane and Father Grannal had created the Lithgow Shamrocks the year before. Even though they'd been in town for a while, they were priests we'd never had anything to do with. The Shamrocks were a bit of a joke. The Workmen's Club was much stronger.

Mum spoke. 'Wherever he plays is up to me, Father. I know he's being considered for state selection later this year, he might get offers from some stronger clubs.'

Father Kane was wounded. 'I'd be very disappointed if he chose to play for Workies, Mrs Slaven. The Shamrocks play with Catholic values.'

Father Keogh joined in. 'It's a totally Catholic-values club, Mrs Slaven. Father Grannal will be conducting a special mass for the team. I'll be making the announcement shortly. It's all going to be very exciting. Sister Francis is writing a club theme song as we speak, isn't that right, Father? Sister Francis, isn't it?'

'Sister Francis indeed, Father. A most talented nun. Loves her football.'

Mum rattled about with the jug and tea was poured.

'Mrs Slaven, I've brought Father Kane to meet you because he has done a lot of very good parish work dealing with single mothers. Now, before you get your hackles in a knot, hear us out. It's clear to the parish that Mr Slaven is unlikely to return, which makes you especially vulnerable to exploitation. Isn't this right, Father?'

Father Kane nodded.

'In my experience, Mrs Slaven, without a man about, the moral rudder on the ship of soul can become loose.'

Father Keogh looked at me. 'It might be a good idea if you go outside and occupy yourself, Roy, this is a time just for the adults. Understand me, now?'

Mum glared at them. I stood my ground.

Father Kane continued. 'I've heard about the womenfolk at the Berlei factory. The wearing of the miniskirt and the paint on the face and the parading of themselves like pieces of meat before men who know no better. You have heard of a Petri dish, Mrs Slaven, a Petri dish is where germs and viruses gather and the Berlei factory is a Petri dish for sin. This is a fact known to all. My advice is to contact your husband, remind him of his financial duties to you and Roy and the church and the parish, and either join him in the parish of Caragabal or encourage him to return to his family. It is imperative that you leave the Berlei factory where temptation is everywhere.

'And I hear you are doing shiftwork! Leaving a young, impressionable boy free to roam the streets at night looking for mischief. For the sake of the boy, Mrs Slaven, I implore you to come back to the mass. Come back to the church. Let's fix the rudder on your ship of soul. The rudder, Mrs Slaven.' And he used his hand as a rudder. 'The rudder. Let's set it right. Let's steer our soul towards the grace of Jesus Christ, the son of God, whose light can only be clearly seen through the holy prism of the Holy Catholic Church and its sacraments.'

Father Keogh nodded. 'Amen.' Then added, 'Why don't we all now kneel and say a decade of the rosary, eh? Then maybe Father Kane might hear your confession.'

'Very happy to do so.' Father Kane removed his stole from his briefcase and placed it around his neck while Father Keogh took his rosary beads from his pocket.

Mum looked at me. I knew she'd had enough.

Father Keogh pressed on. 'Father, tell her about poor Betty Piggott.'

Father Kane paused and shook his head. 'Ah. A very sad case it was, it was. Married young. Too young, of course. Had no control of her emotions and of course her husband, a decent and caring man, was forced by circumstance to find work away from the happy little village in which they were, by the good grace of God, so lucky to find themselves. Well, as time went by —'

'Stop. Please. I don't want to be rude, Fathers, but I suspect I'm going to be.'

Father Kane could not be stopped. 'Mrs Slaven, Betty Piggott was the same as you. At first hostile, she was. She had such an anger, Mrs Slaven, an unhealthy anger that was clearly the work of the devil.'

Mum jumped in. 'Fathers, I am not Betty Piggott. And if you were to ask me am I interested in the plight of Betty Piggott, I am not. And I'm going to ask you both to leave now. I am not having my confession heard now, I'm not. And you know why? Because I am arrogant enough to say to you both, with Roy here as my witness, that to my certain knowledge I am not in a state of sin. Why my husband has left is as much a mystery to me as it probably is to him. He's the one with the problems, Fathers, not me. My problems are the same as any woman trying to make ends meet under very trying circumstances. And for you to suggest that my son is somehow roaming the streets at night looking for trouble is to not know my son at all. And to not know me.'

She made her way to the front door and opened it. The priests looked at each other and crabbed their way out.

Mum closed the door. She looked at me. 'Roy, you have got to make me a promise.'

I nodded.

'Promise me you will never contemplate joining the priesthood.'

I said, 'I think that's a pretty easy promise to make, Mum.' And she ruffled my hair.

'We'll be fine, Roy. We'll be fine.' Then she looked at me again and shook her head. Her breathing was heavy.

•

Mum went to the RSL Club on Saturday night. For the first time. It was the weekend after the two priests had dropped in. Mum paraded herself before me in the lounge room. 'How do I look?'

'Mum, you look beautiful. Like a film star.'

She did, too. I'd never seen her in high heels. It made her nearly as tall as me. Her hair was up in a swirling roll. She wore a stole that set off the turquoise dress she had made. She kissed me on the forehead. 'And you smell nice, Mum.' She twirled once, theatrically, and glided out of the house. Kathy Wilson picked her up in a Vauxhall Velox.

I had a tin of sardines on toast and four boiled eggs for tea, and at about eight o'clock, I cycled over to Doyle's place.

I'd never been to Doyle's before. They had a shop called a 'mixed business' that was attached to the house. I entered the shop and he told me he was closing up and to meet him out the back. I rode around the back lane and entered the yard, which was busy with stacked boxes of soft drinks and a really big coal bin. There was only just room for a car. After a few minutes he appeared at the back door and called me in.

There were doors everywhere. We went into the kitchen. The television was on in the lounge room but you could sit by the door in the living room that led to the back of the shop and watch the screen. He asked me to give him a hand and led me down into the shop. We passed by large bags of potatoes and shelves that reached to the ceiling stacked with boxes of products from Rinso to Lux soap, to tissues to Rice-a-Riso, and a wall of Arnott's biscuit tins of every description. There was a large bench with a machine that sliced meats. Then we were behind the refrigerators and there was another door that led out to the front yard.

He wanted me to help him shift three large metal milk crates filled with pint bottles of milk into the shop. He placed the milk bottles into the fridge. I passed them to him. Then we lugged the empty crates back out into the front yard. Then he took all the takings out of the till and put the money into a white bag. I couldn't believe how much stuff there was. He opened a fridge door and told me to take a bottle of soft drink. 'Have whatever you like,' he said. I grabbed a medium bottle of Coke. He didn't have anything.

We went back up into the house. He said he wouldn't be long. He went into the lounge room and I could see his grandmother. She was on a lounge chair beside the piano. She had a speaker to her ear. The speaker was attached by a cable to the television. On the lounge sat his sister, Jen. She was rocking. Really vigorously. Doyle said something to her and she stopped and said, 'All right,' in a flat toneless voice. She stood and flapped her arms about wildly and then screwed her hands up under her chin. She looked at me, but didn't see me. Or wasn't interested in me. Doyle led her through to what I took to be the bedrooms.

I looked about. There were paintings on the wall. Sherb would have liked them because they all had gum trees. Landscapes. There was a radiogram in the corner. A few family photos were here and there. I sipped my Coke.

Then he's back behind me; he's used another door. 'Ma will be going to bed soon and we can listen to some records.' He led me back towards the corridor that led to the back door, opened yet another door and switched on the light. 'This is my study,' he said. 'The beer room.'

It was a small room. Lino floor. Every wall was stacked with cases of DA. He had fashioned a desk using a piece of timber that straddled even more beer cases. Some books stood in rows across the boxes. On the 'desk' were some exercise books, a few textbooks I recognised, a small tape recorder and leaning against some other cases was a bass guitar. We sat on the floor and talked about the cricket matches we'd played that afternoon. He was happy with five wickets for thirty-seven in the men's B grade and I was happy with one hundred and nineteen, not out, in the A grade.

He had a transistor radio, which he put on. 2LT was doing requests. We didn't listen to the music, but stopped our conversation to hear the requests. One was for Vicki Westwood from Flynn. He'd requested 'The Letter' by The Box Tops.

'Not a bad choice,' I said.

Doyle shook his head. 'Brewer's done that. "The Letter" is the one song Vicki Westwood hates.'

Doyle said he was waiting for a request he'd put in.

'This is 2LT, the sweet sound of the glorious gateway to the central west, and I'm Terry Preece and we're taking your requests all the way up to the top of the hour. This is a song for you, Kay Green. It's from your special friend Jim Keogh and it's, of course, 'The Last Waltz'. You've got to love Engelbert. Enjoy it, Kay Green.'

I cacked myself. It had never occurred to me that you could do that. 'What if someone finds out?' I asked.

He shrugged. 'How could they?'

Then the door opens and a very old woman is standing there with a walking stick. 'Have you done the milk crates, John?'

'Yes, Ma. Ma, this is Roy. I play cricket with him.'

'You spend too much time on cricket. I've left the television set on for you.'

'Okay, Ma. Sleep well.'

'I wish,' she says.

Then Doyle gets up. 'Come on,' he says to me.

He turns the television off and grabs the phone book. He gives it to me and tells me to look up a number. Anyone. While I do that he gets a forty-five out and places it on the turntable in the radiogram. 'Got a number?'

'Umm, yeah. How about Abbott, B?'

'Sounds okay to me. What's the number?'

'Two-three-two-one.'

He picks up the phone. Dials. Eventually someone answers. 'Oh hello, Mrs Abbott, is it? Good. I'm Terry Preece from 2LT and we're running a competition.' He listens. 'Terrific. Okay, now I'm going to play a few bars from a song and if you can identify it, then you can pick up an LP record from Art Boots in town.'

He stands and puts the needle arm on the turntable. It's 'Penny Lane'. He lets it play for about three seconds, before lifting the arm off and says, 'Well, Mrs Abbott?' He listens. 'Yes, that's right. Congratulations! Now I want you to present yourself at Art Boots next Saturday morning between ten and ten-thirty and you can collect the LP of your choice. And remember, keep listening to the sweet sounds of the central west.' And he hangs up. Then we laugh.

'We've got the bye next week, we could go and watch her collect her prize.' We cack ourselves.

'What if we . . . get caught?'

'How?'

He puts *Revolver* on. We find we have quite a bit in common. We'd sort of known each other all our lives but had never really talked. We were born on the same day. We love sport. We hate the same Brothers. We like the same Brothers. We both have issues with the church. We know Father Keogh is weird. We both wonder what the Brothers get up to when school's out. We're both worried about Brother Michael being really lonely. We generally hate Publics. Doyle reckons there are some good ones. 'There are a couple of Publics in my brother's band,' he says. 'They're lovely blokes. Funny. They've got stories of what life's like out there, you know? It's another world out there.' I knew what he meant. We agreed Mr Hammond's a nice bloke, and fair. He said he'd spoken to Flynn about what it was like to sit with the Publics at the pool. 'He said it was like having a veil removed.'

'A veil? What sort of veil?'

Doyle considers. 'When I've played at the club with Dad, and with Uncle Ray . . . they become different people. They talk about things that are taboo. They don't do that at home. I played at the bowling club two weeks ago with Uncle Ray. The drummer is George Eckford. He'd be . . . as old as Ma.

But he can still play. We're having a break between brackets and the piano player, Alan Gemmett, casually says to George, "George, when did you first have sex?" George thinks. He says, "When I was five." We nod. Then he says, "Correction. Four." And everybody laughs. It's funny. Publics can be really funny. Maybe that's what Flynn means by veil. There are no taboos. Remember how friendly and funny Janet was when we sat with her and Vicki Westwood and Flynn?'

We both envy Flynn's ability to relate to girls. Doyle likes Sonia, O'Brien's girlfriend. I do, too. Flynn introduced them. Doyle didn't know that but it didn't surprise him. 'Flynn knows more girls than anyone.'

Doyle has a theory about Flynn. 'He's able to be himself when he's with girls. I don't know about you, but I can't do that. I try to make myself more interesting than I am. I can't help it. If I was to just be myself with a girl she'd be bored shitless.'

I say I thought I was myself when I was with Susan Morgan.

'And O'Brien's himself when he's with Sonia,' Doyle says.

'True.'

We both like O'Brien. We agree he's the most easygoing bloke we knew.

'I've played a lot of footy with O'Brien and I've never seen him lose his temper. And the high school blokes really serve it up to him. He's like a V8 Customline. He just keeps going.'

'God, he's quick, though. More like a Ferrari.'

Then the talk turns to Harold. We agree Harold is somehow different. If O'Brien is a Ford Customline, Harold is a hotted-up

Ford Anglia. Just weird. He likes to hit us across the back of the head. Or use his knuckles on our heads. 'It's all about the head with Harold,' says Doyle.

We both have seen Harold at night sitting alone in his Volkswagen. 'What's he up to, do you think?' I ask.

'I think if I was living with Jack, I'd spend a fair bit of time in the car.'

I'm tempted to tell Doyle about the betting business and having to get out on twenty-one, but think better of it. Then Doyle says, 'Dean's seen his needle. He told Dean it was for heroin.'

'What does heroin do?'

'Dunno. It can't make you happy. Harold's never happy.'

We agreed we had never seen Harold laugh at anything. He always looks annoyed. 'Dean said his mother said that you can get by okay on heroin. Supply is the problem. It's illegal. He said his mum thought the needle was more likely for steroids than heroin. But I think he's the best teacher we've got. I always enjoy periods with Harold. He knows his stuff. He doesn't bullshit and play games. He actually teaches.'

'What do steroids do?'

'Make you bigger or something. They make you better at sport.'

Having opened the innings with Harold in A grade for two seasons I'd seen him up close. 'He's funny to open with. He talks all the time. Comes down to me. "No hooking, okay? Keep it straight. And don't try the cut until we know what the ball's doing." I just ignore it. Listen and ignore it. But it doesn't stop.'

Doyle says, 'He's just making sure he has his mind on the job. He's easily distracted. He's definitely odd.'

I suggest that it's heroin that makes Harold sit in the dark in his car. We list the streets we've seen him in. There are only two. Hassans Walls Road, down near Queen Elizabeth Park, and Main Street near the Theatre Royal.

Doyle points out that both roads border the park. 'Maybe he likes looking at the park.' We decide that Harold's world only makes sense when seen through the eyes of heroin or steroids, so we would never know.

Doyle picks up the phone. 'Two-three-two-one, wasn't it?' He dials. It's answered. 'Mrs Abbott?' A pause. 'Constable Eric Smith. Mrs Abbott, we have every reason to believe students from Lithgow High School have been making prank calls pretending to be representing radio station 2LT.' He listens. 'That's right,' he says. 'I'm sorry this has happened. We are confident we know who the culprits are. Yes, it's a sorry state of affairs. Goodnight, Mrs Abbott.' He hangs up. Moves to the kitchen.

He gets the frying pan out. 'Would you like a toasted sandwich?'

'That'd be great.' And he makes a ham, cheese and tomato toasted sandwich. Adds mustard. It doesn't take long. It's a practised hand.

He turns the television on and we sit, side by side. Errol Flynn is *Gentleman Jim*. It's the best toasted sandwich ever.

Two pigs in a pod.

Just before I leave, Doyle confides in me that he was Susan Morgan's boyfriend back in fourth class. For weeks. And I realise, I knew that.

•

I ride back home, getting in near midnight. It's starting to get a bit cold so I light the fire. I'm a bit agitated. I don't feel tired. I wish we had a television. Or a radio. And then I have the idea that maybe I could get a job. Something part-time. Flynn had a job. I think O'Brien might.

I needed to find out how much a television set cost. And an antenna. Maybe a radio first. It was tricky with television. You could be in a spot where there was no reception. Brewer could get Nine and Two, but his neighbours got Seven and Two. There was a relay station at Orange, CBN8, but nobody thought it was much good. Doyle got Nine, Ten and Two, but he said Ten was pretty ordinary. But he watched a lot of television. He really liked a show called *Danger Man* on Channel Nine.

There's movement at the door. Mum's home. She floats into the room with her high heels in her hands and takes up her favoured position in front of the fireplace. She's a bit tipsy. 'They're lovely people, Roy. I've had a wonderful night.'

I'm keen to hear the details.

'Well. It was a dinner dance. There was so much choice for dinner. I had roast lamb and baked vegetables, but I could have had Chinese. It was a good crowd, not many Catholics, and I sat with Kathy's friends. Two of them were teachers, one worked at Fosseys and Debbie was there from Berlei's. And yes, I got up and had a dance, with a pimply kid who works at Finley's. The band was fantastic. Tony Doyle's band. He can play so many instruments. And he sings. I had no idea. I got to meet them. Honestly, Roy, it's the most fun I've had in . . .' Mum was nearly teary. I asked her if she wanted a cup of Milo or something but she said she'd better get to bed.

'How was your night?' she asked as she headed off.

'Good, Mum. Mucked about with Doyle. It was good. The House of Doors.'

•

I went to the eight-thirty mass. Father Keogh was pretty wound up about Communism. 'They're coming. Mark my words. The fact of the matter is, Communism is here already. In the trade unions. And the number one enemy of the Communists? Catholics! They have a plan to banish Our Lord Jesus Christ from our lives. They will ban our schools, burn down all our churches and torture any one of us that continues to practise our faith. They will torture our children, the elderly, no one will be spared. We have a duty to be continually mindful of what these perpetrators of evil are up to. And they must be stopped. It's in Russia, in the soviet socialist republics, in China, in South East Asia and it is a cancerous festering plague that is heading our way. Australia is under attack. Catholics must unite. We must say enough! In the name of the Lord Jesus Christ and the holy apostolic church.'

Susan Morgan was there. We caught each other's eye during the sermon and met up behind the sacristy when mass was over. Her family was leaving for Mittagong that day. I wanted to kiss her, but there were too many people about and it wouldn't have been right. She was really upset at leaving and really upset because her brother, Michael, had been called up. I didn't know she had a brother. She said she'd write to me and I said I'd write to her, but we both knew we probably wouldn't.

Then her father's behind her. 'For God's sake, come on, Susan.' And she turns and she's gone.

A light had gone out in Lithgow.

•

On my way home I found a *Lithgow Mercury* that had been left on a bench in Queen Elizabeth Park. It would tell me the cost of a television. Four hundred and sixty-nine dollars for a twenty-inch. It was never going to happen. Mum was on one dollar and fifteen cents an hour at Berlei's. Less than fifty dollars a week. Less tax. I'd have to rob a bank.

I'd explore getting a radio. I'd ask Doyle for advice.

•

In the paper, I noticed that a bloke called Thomas Anderson from Rylstone was refusing to go to Vietnam. He'd been called up, but was claiming he was 'a conscientious objector'. It was against his faith to kill, even in war. He was going to court. I thought it might be an avenue Susan's brother could explore. I raised the issue with Brother Connor the next day.

'Yes, Slaven?'

'Brother, what's a conscientious objector?'

Brother Connor thought about this. 'A conscientious objector, Slaven?'

'Yes, Brother.'

Brother Connor paces. 'Slaven, imagine you and your mum are sitting in your lounge room having a very jolly old time and someone barges into your home threatening to kill your mum. What would you do?'

'Umm . . . try to stop him.'

'Yes, I think you would. And if in stopping him, you killed him, would you be guilty of murder, Slaven?'

'I don't think so, Brother.'

'No, I don't think so either. Your actions would be justified. And that's the key. Justified. Now, what if you had sat back and let this scoundrel murder your mother? Not bothered to lift a finger?'

'Umm . . .'

'The question is not rhetorical, Slaven. You would be seen as being cowardly, correct?'

'Probably.'

'See, you can conscientiously object to participation in war if the war is not justified.' Brother Connor wandered about the room. 'So. What you are asking is whether the war in Vietnam is justified. If it is justified then you have the same responsibility to act on behalf of the nation as you would in beating off your mother's attacker. Clear?'

I nodded.

'It's the motive of the so-called conscientious objector that I would question. Imagine in our Rugby League team we have a cove with a philosophical objection to tackling. I'd call that cove a coward. Now, many of you would be aware that the South Vietnamese Prime Minister Air Vice-Marshal Ky has been a visitor to our shores, and what an impressive fellow he is. He wants our help to fend off those who are trying to force a Communist way of life upon his people. There are many, many Catholics in South Vietnam who will be slaughtered should the Communists win. We have a duty, do we not?' He looked at us all. 'I will have no further talk of conscientious objection in this classroom. Understood?'

Then Brewer put his hand up. 'Should Ronald Ryan have been hanged, Brother?'

Ronald Ryan had divided the community much in the manner of Ned Kelly.

Brother Connor looked at Brewer squarely. 'We pray for his soul, boys. It's a tragedy. Especially for the young policeman he shot. We pray for the family of the policeman. But I cannot accept capital punishment. And nor can the church.'

Now Dean had his hand up.

'Yes, Dean?'

'Should Catholics vote for Aboriginals to be given the vote?'

'Dean. That is such a silly question. Of course Catholics should vote yes. It's a national embarrassment that they haven't been able to. Racism. Pure and simple. Enough distractions.'

•

I saw Doyle at lunchtime and asked him about radios. He said we should see his uncle at Finley's. 'Finley's for fine furniture.' So, after school, we rode into Main Street and went into Finley's. It smelled new. It was the first time I'd been in a big store like this. Furniture everywhere. Lounge suites and wardrobes and televisions and radiograms and transistor radios and toys and guns, all made larger by the reflections in the many mirrors. Doyle wandered up the back. His uncle was the manager of the store and together they joined me in the television area. His Uncle Ray was a tall bloke, quietly spoken and really friendly. Doyle called him 'Unc'. He loved his Rugby League and was right behind the Shamrocks. And he liked to talk. 'Aren't you the young bloke no one can get out?'

I nodded.

'Unc, do people trade in their old radios? Roy needs a radio.'

'Follow me,' he said and we went downstairs where the smell of glue was really pungent. He said it was because Reg was joining some Axminster together for a job at Oaky Park and then he led us into a room stacked with old furniture. He rooted around, shifting lounges and chairs, and found a radio on the floor. He picked it up to show me. It was a Philips BX 453.

'It's a 1950 model. Good brand. It's good quality Bakelite, should have a reasonable sound.' And he wiped it with a cloth from his pocket and carried it upstairs and set it up in his office. He plugged it in. 'It'll take a little while for the valves to warm up.' And, sure enough, after a few moments and a bit of fiddling with a knob, 2LT came to life.

'What's it worth, Unc?'

Ray Doyle looked at me, looked back at the radio and said, 'Well, you know, today's a special day. Today we're offering a five finger discount.'

I didn't know what he meant.

'Take it home with you. Just make sure when you need some furniture down the track, you come to Finley's.'

I looked at Doyle. He nodded.

'Are you sure, Mr Doyle?'

'Call me, Ray. I tell you what, I wouldn't trust you to get it home on your bike. I'll drop it off on my way home from work if you like. Be about ten past six. I know where you live, you're Bot's boy, aren't you?'

It was the only time I was happy to be called Bot's boy.

I was in a state of disbelief.

That night, I waited outside the house looking at all the cars turn the corner into our street, which was pretty busy. At about half past six a blue and cream Holden Special pulls up. It's Mr Doyle. He winds the window down. 'It's on the back seat behind me, Roy.'

I took it out of the car. 'Thanks, Mr Doyle. Mum'll be —'

'You've got to look after your mother, mate,' he said. 'Any news of your Dad?'

I shook my head.

He nodded. 'Happy listening!' Then he drove off.

I set it up in the kitchen and we had music in the house. I couldn't wait for Mum to get home. She was a bit tired when she got in but she gave me the biggest smile. I told her the story. She said Mr Doyle was a lovely man. There was some sort of swing music playing, might have been Duke Ellington, and Mum made me have a dance with her, old-fashioned style. I trod on her foot. She didn't mind. She laughed.

Chapter Eight

'Benson, your only role in life is to waste my time.'
BROTHER CONNOR

'Benson, you could catch fire and be the last to know.'
BROTHER CONNOR

Brother Michael was at a loose end. It was a Thursday afternoon. He was looking for someone to play tennis with. Dean and Doyle were playing and Doyle said he had a spare racquet. It suited me. So we agreed to meet at the Littleton courts, which were free, at about four o'clock. I had played tennis once before with Uncle Baz in Cowra. He was a good player.

I'd played a lot of backyard tennis with Mum. We used bats Dad made out of plywood. Mum was a really good volleyer. We would sometimes volley to each other for hours. Dad just liked hitting the ball hard, which was less interesting. Mum liked to talk about 'touch'. In our backyard competitions, the final was always between me and Mum. We both could beat Dad easily.

But the big court was a different game.

The balls were pretty old and I partnered Brother Michael. The racquet Doyle had lent me was a Spalding Pancho Gonzales. I'd never heard of Pancho Gonzales. Brother Michael had. He said he was a champion.

We started off having a hit. Doyle wasn't bad. Dean had no control. Brother Michael was very keen and chased everything down. More often than not, he got the ball back. And he laughed a lot. He loved tennis. Loved being out of the Brothers' house. Lithgow was his first appointment. He was a big kid. An elder brother for us all.

We were having a good match. I found that I could control the ball pretty well. I started experimenting with top-spin.

Brother Michael was astonished. He stopped the match. 'Show me how you did that, Roy.'

He got Doyle to hit a few balls to me and I found I could hit the ball really hard; the top-spin kept the ball from flying and increased the accuracy. 'It's in the timing, Brother. You've got to watch the ball onto the strings. You throw the racquet at the ball.' He had a go, with mixed results, but was determined to master the technique.

Eventually, we had to stop. It was getting dark. Brother Michael said he'd like to play regularly. I said it suited me, so we started playing singles together every Thursday for a while. The top-spin proved too difficult for him to master, but I enjoyed putting the ball where I thought he would like it and we had some rallies that lasted thirty shots or more. He really loved it. He asked me about Dad a lot, but I had nothing to add. Father goes to Caragabal shearing. End of story.

'Does he ever write? To your mother?'

'No, Brother. No letters.'

He found it baffling. He was troubled by it.

He told me he was worried about Sherb. We all were, I said. I told him about the rubber club he was using.

'Ah,' he said. 'You've solved the mystery. We wondered what had happened to the flooring. Brother Hugh was considering calling the police in, he thought it must have been done by vandals. I'll have a word to Brother Connor about it. He'll know the best way to approach it.'

Then we just sat in the cabana for a moment, as the darkness fell. The soft wind was blowing the scent of the pines from the pine forest. 'We think it's his heart. He has a weak heart. He needs our prayers.'

I took this in.

•

I decided that I'd go to benediction on Friday night as an offering for Sherb because, despite his madness, I liked him. Everybody liked him. He'd been teaching for so long, seen so many of us passing through, going somewhere, growing. We must be all the same to him. He once called O'Brien Arnold. Arnold is his father's name. And Flynn was often Bill. Same deal. Sometimes he called me Cec. There were a lot of Slavens in Lithgow. They were a very sporting family and great contributors to the community. The Slavens became the heart of the Shamrocks. There were plenty of Slavens at De La Salle and there must have been a Cec at some stage, years ago. I was a Cowra Slaven. Different family.

Dad was born in Cowra. Uncle Baz is still there, and Dad has a sister there, Kathleen. We never see Kathleen because her husband Boxhead Keenan told Dad that the next time he sees him he's going to kill him. I think Dad had taken the threat pretty seriously, but I don't know what he did. Nor does Mum. So she says.

Benediction was okay. I thought of Sherb a lot. Asked Our Lord to look after him and make him strong. And I studied the Children of Saint Mary. Girls our age and older wore blue gowns and white veils and sat together in the first row of pews, with a couple of the girls' mothers and Sister Valerian. Margot was there. And Deirdre. And Anne. Two of the Cullen girls. What the Sisters of Mary got up to, I have no idea. Sister Geraldine kept glancing at me and at the end of the service approached me and asked if I'd like a cup of tea.

She was middle-aged. Tall. The starched part of the habit that gripped her face was kind to her. When she smiled she was vivacious. Instantly likeable.

I walked with her to the convent, a stately Victorian two-storey building across the road from the church, and she led me through the front door. Through the first door to the right was a sitting room. She asked me to sit down and then jangled down the hall to the kitchen. I sat.

It was pretty quiet. Very sparse. Just like we have it at home, but this was much, much neater. No dust. After five minutes I hear her jangling back and she has a tray she places on the small table. The tray has a small tea service and a small plate with two scotch finger biscuits on it. She pours the tea as she plies me with questions. 'And you're the sportsman, aren't you?'

'I do like sport, Sister.'

'What do you like about it?'

'It's easy. It's fun. I think I see things a lot of blokes don't.'

'You're not talking visions?'

'No, Sister. Not visions. Signs.'

'What signs?'

'Okay. Cricket. I can tell where the ball will bounce from the moment it leaves the bowler's hand. Brian Booth told me not to try to analyse it. And I can see where the seam is on the ball and how it's spinning. Then I know where I'm going to hit it. Sometimes I get a better idea and hit it somewhere else. But I control it.'

She seemed really interested.

'Rugby League? I can tell where someone is going to run, where they'll be in two or three seconds' time. Two seconds is plenty of time to adjust and plan where to throw the ball. I can see the gaps. The poor players give me three seconds, the really good ones, two.' I don't think she's following this. She's glazing over. So I shut it down. 'Anyway . . .'

She grabs the moment and says urgently, 'I'm going to be joint principal with Brother Hugh next year. Brother Hugh likes sport.'

'Loves it, Sister. He's our footy coach. He's a fully qualified referee. He refs first grade. Group ten.'

'But, like me, he's from Melbourne.'

'Yes, Sister.'

'I can't stand Rugby League. Can't bear it. I don't understand it at all. I like Aussie Rules.'

I'd never heard of Aussie Rules. There was a game at school called 'Salle Rules', which was just forcing. You'd punt the ball as far as you could and, wherever it was caught, it would be punted back by the bloke who caught it. Maybe it was a bit like that.

I took a biscuit. It was stale. She stared straight at me. 'I know he plays cricket. I've tried talking to him about cricket, but . . .' She shrugged.

'He can't talk to women, Sister. He goes weird.'

She sits up. Her mouth is open. 'It's not just me?'

'No, Sister. You should talk to my mum about him. Mum can't get . . . Mum just gets strange noises.'

'That's it!' Her relief was palpable. I can see she's thinking now. I wash down the last of the biscuit with the last of the tea.

She nods. 'Thank you so much, Roy. The problem is much larger than we thought. Don't often see you at benediction.'

I say I was there for Sherb. She says she'll talk to Brother Hugh about Brother Hubert next time she sees him.

'I'm so grateful for your intelligence,' she says, then she stands and shows me out. 'We must make this a habit.' And she winks at me.

I had been initiated into the special group of those who had been invited to have a cup of tea with Sister Geraldine at the convent. O'Brien was one. Doyle was another. And now there was me.

Had to blow on my hands on the way home on the bike. Autumn was blowing me a kiss.

•

Flynn said he had some work delivering newspapers. *The Clarion* came out every Saturday. It was a free newspaper published in Burns Lane just off Main Street. It gave an alternative view and was as much focused on international issues as it was on local ones. Flynn said I should join him and see how it's done, on the off-chance a bit of work might come up. So I did.

George Gearside made Sherb look like a boy. He was a one-man industry. Wrote most of the articles, did the typesetting, worked the press. Thin. Wiry. Thick glasses. Blue overalls, with a small pencil behind his ear and he was deaf. He was deaf because the machinery in the corrugated-iron, brick-floored factory is loud. Very, very loud.

At three o'clock, when I put my head around the door to find Flynn, Mr Gearside is shouting something I don't understand at a man I learn is his seventy-year-old son, George Junior. George Junior nods.

Flynn is collecting piles of newspapers as they gather at the bottom of the printing press and running them onto a bench. 'Give us a hand,' he yells. So I do, and within minutes my ears are ringing. Then George Junior pulls a huge lever and there is silence. My ears keep ringing for minutes.

Then we're rolling newspapers and putting elastic bands around them. There's no small talk. Mr Gearside supervises. His son rolls with us. George Junior is very slow. I get into a rhythm and soon I'm doing five times the number of newspapers of Flynn and the son combined.

George Junior stops and watches me. He says, 'You fuck'n smart shit. You're going to give him ideas.'

Then Mr Gearside shouts, 'What? What did you say?'

George Junior says, 'Nothin'.'

Mr Gearside steps towards us. 'Are you watching this? He's good, this one. You both should try doing it like he does.' Then to me, 'You're Bot's boy.'

I nod.

'I'm so bloody glad you didn't take after him. He's fucked off, hasn't he? Complete turd, Bot.' Then he walks off.

At four o'clock, we're in an old Ford Customline, windows down, throwing the rolled newspapers into people's front yards. George Junior drives. He sings 'Melancholy Baby.' It was fun at first but quickly got pretty boring. He knew all the words to 'Melancholy Baby'. We do this for three and a half hours. Flynn and I will be able to recite all the words to 'Melancholy Baby' for the rest of our lives.

It's eight o'clock by the time we get back to the factory. Then Flynn gets paid. One dollar and fifteen cents. It would take hundreds of years to get a television set. A couple of weeks later Flynn said there was some work for me. I said I wasn't going to do it. 'Too hard,' I said.

He nodded. 'I'll ask Brewer.'

•

I'm standing with Dean, Doyle, Benson and Brewer under the imposing pine trees beside what used to be two tennis courts, which is now the main playground for the school. O'Brien joins us. He tells us that Miss Australia is in town. He says her name is Margaret Rohan. Then Flynn joins us. Flynn knows she'll be visiting Bracey's this afternoon. Bracey's is a department store. Sells a lot of clothes. Brewer says she must be the most beautiful woman in Australia. Benson says he'd like to have a look at her. Brewer said he'd like to know what Flynn could tell about her. So we decide we'll meet at Bracey's after school.

We all turn up. Even Dean. We hang around outside the store. Across Main Street a group of Publics is gathering around the Bluebird Café. They are about the same age as us. Hammond is among them. I judge them harmless. They judge us as harmless. They're probably here for the same reason we are. To see the most beautiful woman in Australia.

Eventually, a Chrysler Royal parks in the bus stop, a driver gets out and opens the back door, and Miss Australia gets out of the car. There are wolf-whistles from the Publics. She is beautiful. We stay silent, holding our bikes, eyes glued on her as she is escorted right past us into Bracey's. She is dressed for an opening night in Hollywood. Her appearance, her deportment:

impeccable. She seems unknowable. We look at Flynn. He nods. And we all know she's had a root.

•

Flynn said he was related to Errol Flynn. He said it was a fact that Errol Flynn had had more roots than any man in history. Dean said, 'What about Genghis Khan?' Flynn said Errol's record 'shits all over that loser'. He said that Errol wore trousers that had been specifically tailored to meet the requirements of his cock. There was a special pouch attached to the gusset that reached almost to the top of his left sock. Flynn felt this family connection gave him a particular insight into all matters concerning sex, the opposite sex and pregnancy.

And pregnancy was in the air. *The Clarion* that I was given when I helped Flynn had an article that argued birth control was a good thing. Mum read it. But the Pope was arguing that any artificial birth control was sinful. The 'rhythm' method was the church's recommendation for those who wanted to engage in sex with a reduced chance of pregnancy. Flynn was the expert on all these matters.

We were eating lunch near the toilets by the oval. Tropics and Tundra together. Flynn was holding court. 'It takes most people eight roots to get pregnant.' He was eating two buttered Weet-Bix bound together with newspaper. 'Unless you're Errol. With Errol, it's one root.'

Brennan thought it was bullshit. 'You can get pregnant without rooting.'

'How?' Brewer is involved.

Doyle says, 'Our Lady got pregnant. She didn't have a root.'

Brennan is validated.

'But that's a miracle,' says Brewer.

Dean says his mother, being a nurse, sees a miracle like that every week.

Flynn is keen to steer the conversation back to the wellspring. 'Errol liked to have a root while he watched television. That's a fact. Errol once had a root while he was getting petrol. That's a fact.'

Benson giggled. 'Did he ever have a root at mass?'

It was the funniest thing ever said by anyone in all of history. The Tropics and the Tundra erupted in unison. The sheer naughtiness was magnificent.

It was the greatest moment of Benson's life. He lit up a fag. He didn't care if he was caught.

He wasn't.

•

At assembly, Brother Hugh announced that half the school playground was out of bounds for the foreseeable future. Building was about to begin. The school was getting three new classrooms and an administration block. Most of the work would be done during holidays at the end of term. There would be fundraising, starting with a school fete on a Sunday. Parents were asked to contribute cakes and toffees. 'Bring your money, boys, every little bit helps.'

I spoke to Mum about it, but she didn't seem all that interested. On the day though, she fished through her purse and gave me two dollars.

Doyle arrived at the fete with a beer carton filled with chocolate bars, O'Brien's mum had made toffees and Brewer had cupcakes. Many parents turned up. I was surprised by how big it was. The mayor was there. For a moment we thought Miss Australia might show, but she didn't.

Mr Goggin had set up a huge barbeque near the tuckshop and was selling sausages wrapped in bread with tomato sauce. Ten cents each. I had two. Most delicious things I have ever eaten. Thought about getting two more, but I was full.

By mid-afternoon there could have been a thousand people there. It was weird seeing girls at the school. The oval was choking with lines of cars. You could buy anything – dresses, tools, you name it. Brother Hugh wandered about looking proud and grinning and, as usual, making really weird noises whenever approached by a woman. 'Ah, Mrs gghhrrgh Dean, gnnnrrrrgh, Mrs Goggin, gghhrrrgh.' And he'd flush red and move off, seeking the comfort of less threatening company.

A microphone and speaker had been organised and the bell rang and there was an official party. Mr Austin took charge and introduced the mayor, and invited the mayoress, Mrs Robson, to officially open the fete. This was a bit weird because the fete had been going for hours. Mrs Robson thanked everyone for being so generous and stressed the need for quality education. Mr Austin thanked her and repeated the message of generosity.

Dean thought it a bit hypocritical that Mr Austin should be there. His son had been in our class in primary school, but had then gone to an expensive private school in Sydney for his secondary education. He thought Mr Austin had shown little faith in the school. He said his mum had said Mr Austin had 'voted with his feet'. Mr Austin had teamed up with Mr Butta to form Austin and Butta, a coal mining and coal transport company, which was very successful. The word was that Mr Austin and Mr Butta were millionaires.

Sister Geraldine was there. She had a word to Doyle and Dean and me. The sun was shining and it was almost windless. She said she'd prayed for fine weather and was relieved that her prayers had been answered. As we were talking, Brother Hugh rounded the corner, saw us, spun around and darted off the way he came. She looked at me and rolled her eyes. She said the science room needed repainting and she was looking for volunteers. Dean said he'd help. So did Doyle. And they agreed to find some time in the holidays.

Flynn and Doyle and I took Deirdre and Barbara, our pool mates, on a tour of the schoolrooms. We showed them where we sit and where Brother Connor stands and how he examines the window frame. They said that if they were with us next year in this room they'd want to be in the Tropics. Even on a warm day like today, the room was freezing.

There was a bit of chalk on the desk and we all wrote our names on the blackboard. Then Flynn drew a dick and balls just like Brother Connor's and explained how spermatozoa swam. I think they thought he was making it up.

Then suddenly Harold's in the room. 'Have you boys seen Jack?'

'I don't think he's here, Sir,' says Doyle.

Harold's a bit agitated. We're worried about the dick and balls on the blackboard and what he might think, but he doesn't see it, or chooses to ignore it. 'Well, that's the last bloody straw,' he says. 'It's a farce. The whole show is a farce. He left me this morning with all the washing up to do. And a bloody basket of clothes to wash. Bloody farce. Honestly, I've got much better things to do than fiddle with Jack's underpants and some pegs.'

Barbara says it's a good day for drying.

'Eh? Good day? No day's a good day for drying, in my book. Not when you've got a new curriculum to write.' And he's gone.

Flynn rubbed the dick and balls off with the duster. Wisely, as it turned out. Sister Pius poked her head in and ordered Barbara and Deirdre out of the classroom. 'You girls know the rules. All girls stay together.'

'Yes, Sister,' they chorused.

The day was deemed a huge success. According to *The Mercury*, a thousand dollars was raised. And that week the timeworn pine trees were cut down and earth-moving equipment started digging the trenches for the footings of the new classrooms.

Chapter Nine

'Your face should be happy, showing
gentleness and respect.'

SAINT JOHN BAPTIST

'To deal with young people very harshly is to
forego all hope of bringing about any good.'

SAINT JOHN BAPTIST

We decided that we were going to be on our best behaviour for Sherb. The Temperate Zone was relieved, because they copped the worst of it when Sherb went 'Das Mayhem'. We'd sit in silence when he came into the classroom. He'd sit and flick through his dog-eared copy of *Around The Boree Log*, stopping at a poem, and then he'd begin to read. We'd stay silent and, after a while, the reading would stop mid-line and he'd be asleep.

One time, Brother Hugh came into the room when Sherb was asleep. He walked up and down each aisle to look at what

we were doing. I was playing hangman with Benson. Doyle
and Dean were doing their Science homework and Brewer was
drawing boats. Marsland was reading a *Phantom* comic, Flynn
Superman and Mahon *Batman*.

Brother Hugh didn't say a word. Nor did he wake Brother
Hubert. He quietly took his leave.

•

Mum was going to the Saturday night dance at the RSL Club
again. Kathy Wilson was picking her up. Mum had made a new
dress that she was really happy with and was in good spirits.
The radio was on pretty well all the time and she liked to
sing along with 'It Must Be Him', in full voice. After fiddling
about in the bathroom, she emerges. She's a symphony of red.
She looks fantastic. There's a toot out the front and she's off.

I had teed up going over to Doyle's and got there a bit after
eight o'clock, just in time to help him with the milk crates.
I chose a bottle of Cottee's Passiona and we settled into his beer
room. He was experimenting with sound effects with his tiny
tape recorder. He'd put some coins in a tin box, pressed record
and shaken the tin and spoken over the din. 'And here comes
Slaven into the middle and just listen to that crowd. Don't they
just love this fellow? He raises his bat in acknowledgement.
Don Bradman is standing. Even Sir Don is calling Slaven,
The Master.' Then he pressed stop, rewind and played it back.
'What do you think?'

It sounded just like the radio.

There's a small tap at the door. It's his youngest sister, Cath. She's about seven years old. 'John. Jen's up.' This is apparently not good news.

I follow them into the lounge room where his grandmother has been watching a movie, looks like a Barbara Stanwyck one. Grandma's on her feet. Jen is in her pyjamas.

She's shouting. And she's violently smashing her face with the back of her hand. His grandma is using her walking stick to try to push Jen's hand away from her face, but she seems to be determined to do herself a terrible damage. Then she's screaming. Doyle tries to steer her away from his grandma, who isn't helping matters at all. Doyle coaxes her into the kitchen, where she bursts into tears. These are tears of some terrible grief.

His grandma sits back down in her lounge chair and puts the speaker back to her ear. Doyle asks Jen if she'd like something to eat, but she's not interested.

'It's Arm!' she screams. 'Arm! Arm! Arm!' And she again attacks her face with the back of her hand. Then she puts her hand behind her head and she's trying to smell her elbow and she says, 'Yes, Arm.' Then she looks at Doyle. 'But why? Why when the yellow tells the, why when the yellow . . . ?' Then she's screaming again. And now she's foaming at the mouth in some monumental rage.

Cath watches the television. Then Jen is cooing and blowing and flapping her hands about and screaming at the ceiling. It's as if she is trying to flee her own body. Doyle watches her while he butters a slice of bread and puts honey on it and cuts it into four squares. 'Come on, mate. This'll be nice.' He presents her with the plate.

'What is it?'

'Honey.'

'But why? Why?'

He says, 'I don't know why, mate. I don't.'

She takes the plate and eats the bread and honey. She hurls the plate at him. It smashes. Cath turns and looks but then returns to the movie.

Doyle gets a broom and tray and sweeps up the plate. Puts it in a bin under the sink. While he does this Jen starts shaking and rocking on her feet from side to side. Her eyes flicker to the ceiling.

'Come on, mate. Back to bed, eh?'

She meekly agrees. He steers her through a doorway and disappears for a couple of minutes. I finish my Passiona. I realise I'm shaking. This has been a real-life horror show.

Doyle reappears. He looks at Cath. 'Yes, mate. Watch the rest of the film, then bed, okay?'

I hear Grandma say, 'Shouldn't you be in bed?'

'She's right, Ma. Mum said she could.' And he winks at Cath and she's happy. He turns to me. 'Come on.' He goes into his beer room and comes out with a packet of Benson & Hedges. We go into the backyard. He lights up a smoke, offers me one. I don't smoke.

'She's autistic,' he says. I ask him what that means. He says he doesn't know. 'Nobody does. That was nothing,' he says. 'She can sometimes scream non-stop for hours. There's nothing you can do but let her wear herself out. But she's declared war on her face. They're trying some medication, but so far nothing's working.'

Seemed weird that she'd be attacking her face, because she was pretty.

Then his grandma is at the back door. 'John, have you done the milk bottles?'

'Yes, Ma. Sleep well.'

'I wish. Cath should be in bed, it's outrageous a girl of that age still up.'

'Yes, Ma. I'll get her to bed now.'

'And what are you doing in the backyard?'

'Looking at the stars, Ma.'

'The stars? What nonsense. You're up to something. You always are.' She makes her way off to her flat attached to the back of the house.

We go back inside. Cath is falling asleep on a lounge chair. Doyle wakes her and tells her to get to bed. She does. He turns the television off.

'Want a sandwich?' A toasted ham, cheese and tomato with mustard is presented and we listen to *Rubber Soul*. Great album. Great sandwich. Weird house.

•

It's just after midnight when I get home and it's turned cold so I light the fire. I realise the whole autistic thing has made me edgy. I can't take the sight of the screaming out of my mind. She was being tortured. By herself. Possessed. By demons.

And then Mum's home. She's pretty wired. She's had a great night. Her dress was a hit and she has two girls coming around tomorrow to get measured up. She says she had the Chinese and wishes she hadn't.

'I think I might have met the most boring man in Australia, tonight. I had to dance with him, would have been rude to say no. He wanted to bring me home. He works at the Commercial Bank. Brian Lawson. Honestly, if he's going to be a regular, I might have to go to the Workies Club.' Then she thinks about it. 'Which would be a real shame. God, the band is good. Alan Oloman from the Black Diamonds sat in for the last bracket. It was just so special. Tony Doyle's brilliant.'

I tell her about Doyle's sister. Try to describe what had happened.

'Oh, the poor thing,' Mum says. 'She's subnormal, isn't she? How old is she?'

'She'd be thirteen or fourteen, I reckon.'

'I have seen her at mass. They sit up the back. Away from prying eyes, I suppose. Must be a terrible drain on Mrs Doyle.'

I nod.

•

On Sunday I went to the footy. The new-look Shamrocks were playing Bathurst St Pat's at the showground. New because they have Stomper Staines in the team. Father Kane and Father Grannal were there. Doyle's Uncle Ray was there. It was a good crowd. I sat in the stand with O'Brien, Benson, Brewer and Flynn.

The Shamrocks played really well. Stomper Staines was outstanding. Best player by a mile. Strong as a bull. I think the only way to stop him is around the legs, which they didn't do. I saw a lot of missed opportunities. They would have one side stacked with players and not use them. And they didn't kick enough in general play. Still. They won, and that's all that mattered.

When I got home I noticed a black Zephyr parked out the front. Red upholstery. Looked like it wanted to be driven fast. When I got in the house there was a tall bloke with wavy black hair having a cup of tea, watching Mum cutting some material on the kitchen table. Mum says, 'Roy, this is Brian.'

Brian says, 'G'day, Tiger. Who won?'

'The Shamrocks.'

'Brian plays tennis. He was telling me he won the A-grade championship.'

Brian grins. 'Straight sets over Tony Nay. Terrific player, Tony. Don't you get the paper? Front page.'

I look at Mum. She gives me a look of helplessness. 'Yes, Brian just happened to be in the area.'

'I had to evaluate a property in Suvla Street. I was just saying to Paulette, most people at the bank just take the market valuation reports at face value. I don't. I think it's best to actually see the property, and I know what you're thinking, valuers know what they're doing, and most times, generally speaking, they do. But I don't want to be the bunny responsible for the bank holding a piece of property that won't ever realise what we've lent out on it. I'm probably a bit over careful, but that's me. More tea, Paulette. Yes, tennis. You learn a lot about yourself with a game like tennis. Do you play, Tiger?'

'Umm . . . not much.'

'No? It requires tremendous discipline. I was talking to Frank Sedgman about it. I used to play with Frank, beat him once. He hated that, just between you and me. He was the number one player in the world. Won Wimbledon and the US Open. Just a fantastic player. He was nearly forty when I played him. Thirty-eight, actually.'

Mum poured some tea from the pot into his cup. He didn't break stride. 'And such a fantastic bloke, Frank Sedgman. So level-headed. Down to earth, you know? He made me realise I was being my own worst enemy. Taught me to believe in my game. And I do. I've met Rod Laver. I call him Rocket. I've met Mr Muscles. Ken Rosewall, to you. Lew Hoad. Lovely player, Lew. I'll take you both to White City sometime. I'm a member there. Sat with Roy Emerson last time I was there. What a funny man. Dry, you know? Very dry. I like a dry sense of humour. We got on like a house on fire.'

It was well after dark when Brian Lawson left. I think he was expecting to be asked to stay for tea. He had some sort of disease, I reckon. He couldn't stop talking. We were standing in the cold air for twenty minutes as he was finally leaving, while he talked about the great deal he got with the Zephyr, and how the radial tyres had improved the cornering. He was the first bloke in Lithgow with radials. Went to Sydney for them. They were imported from Italy. A small factory in Milan.

I looked at Mum as he drove off. 'What am I going to do?' she said.

I was shell-shocked. So was Mum. We had baked beans on toast and listened to the radio and we were both so happy just to be alone. Together.

•

It was Flynn who had the news. Bumper Wright, the Shamrocks' hooker, had died. Just a few hours after the game on Sunday. Flynn said they thought it was a heart attack. We all knew Bumper. He worked at the pool. He was the best hooker in group ten. He'd represented group eleven before moving to Lithgow.

At assembly, Brother Hugh called for a minute's silence. Someone farted. Might have been Benson. It was. Brewer got the giggles. So did Brennan. So did Mahon. Even Dean is shaking. Brother Connor cast an eye over us all. Benson snots himself and gets four when we get into class.

Then Doyle gets one, because Benson could only name one triangle. Then I get two for 'insolence'.

•

Sherb has been taken to hospital. Brother Hugh interrupts Brother Connor's maths lesson to give us the news. Mr Connolly, the Metalwork teacher, will now be taking us for English. We are all deeply concerned about Sherb. Dean says he's at the Lithgow District Hospital. His mum had seen him. Doyle asks if he can have visitors. Dean doesn't know.

Doyle says for me to come around and he'll phone the hospital and see if we can see him.

I drop in after school, around half past four. Knock on the back door. Doyle lets me in and we walk down the hall, pass by the beer room and two other rooms and go through the kitchen into the lounge room. A bell rings. Doyle ignores it. The television is on and his grandma is sitting by the piano with the remote speaker to her ear. Cath sits in another lounge chair watching television. She's eating a bag of potato chips. Jen sits rocking on the lounge.

I can hear a trumpet coming from the bedrooms. Scales. Tony is practising. It's noise everywhere. Whenever the shop door is opened or closed, the bell rings. The bell is on the kitchen wall. Bell. Television. Trumpet. Doyle is telephoning the hospital.

Then from the door to the shop Mrs Doyle comes through, at pace. She gets out some pots from a cupboard and fills each with water. At pace. Then the bell rings and she darts back down into the shop. She doesn't see me at all. Doyle gets off the telephone. We can see Sherb, now.

Doyle catches his mum rushing through the dining room. 'We're going up to see Sherb, Mum.'

'When will you be back?'

'Six.'

'At the latest.' Bell. She's gone.

We rode to the hospital. We pushed our bikes up the last

hundred yards because it's too steep. I'd never been in a hospital before. It had an odd smell. And it was very quiet. The floors were shiny with wax. Doyle talks to a lady behind a counter and we walk past a lot of rooms until we find room eleven.

Sherb is lying in a small bed. His bare feet dangle over the end. Striped pale blue pyjamas. Threadbare. He looks withered. There are three other blokes in his room. They are all old. None of them look well. We shuffle in and stand by Sherb. There are no chairs.

He looks up at us. 'Boys. Might be at the end of the line, boys. But I'm not worried. Lovely of you boys to come. I walked on Sunday. Too far. Hassans Walls. And you know, boys, I felt God was so close. It was almost as if I could reach out and touch Him. I don't fear death, boys. Boys, death is part of life.'

Doyle takes his packet of Benson & Hedges from his pocket. He proffers them to Sherb.

Sherb looks at him. Looks about. 'Did you bring a match, Ray?' Sherb is seeing Doyle as his Uncle Ray. From his pocket, Doyle produces a box of matches. They both light up. Doyle takes the remaining matches out of the box and puts them in his pocket. They use the empty box as an ashtray. 'Tobacco has kept me alive. God's greatest gift to man is the cigarette.'

Sherb dozed off before the cigarette was finished. Doyle took it from his yellowed fingers. He closed the box, put it on the side table and placed some cigarettes in Sherb's pyjama pocket with some matches.

We left.

•

Father Keogh made it clear during the sermon at Sunday's mass that Bumper Wright's death had nothing to do with playing football. 'The Shamrocks football club is blameless. This tragedy was an act of God. And there is a clear lesson here. Death can strike at any time. We must treat each day as if it is our last on this Earth. So ask yourselves, if you were to be called by God today, at this moment, would you be in a state of grace? Ask yourself. Am I worthy of bathing in God's greatness? Have I been the best person I can be? For God has placed a watch inside us all and it's ticking, ticking, ticking. And we know for a certain fact that the time will come when the ticking stops. The ticking will stop for all of us.'

At this point, I noticed many people looked at their watches.

It was a quiet crowd after mass. Usually, it's a boisterous gathering of families holding up the flow through the church doors, but today people just wandered off. I watched Mrs Doyle assist a vigorously flapping Jen into the back seat of the family Valiant. Mr Doyle was already in the car and had the motor running. Jen loudly exclaimed, 'She's going to hit her head.' When she's settled, Cath and Doyle climb in the other side. Doyle sees me and waves. I wave back. There is muffled shouting from the car as it moves off.

I rode over to Brewer's hoping for some scones.

Chapter Ten

'Faith is to believe what you do not see. The
reward of faith is to see what you believe.'
SAINT AUGUSTINE OF HIPPO

'Boys, without faith there is only madness and chaos.'
BROTHER CONNOR

Jack Connolly stood by the blackboard. He looked out of place. We would normally only see him in the metalwork room wearing a long grey coat. He had his hands in his pockets and fiddled with his car keys. 'Boys, hands up those who have a telephone at home.' Six hands go up. 'Dean, let's imagine you are ringing a doctor to make an appointment. Benson, you can take the part of the doctor. Clear? Good. "Bring, bring." That's the phone ringing. "Bring, bring." Better answer it, Doctor.'

'Hello?'

'Is that you, Doctor?'

'Come now. You have cancer.' Laughter.

'Boys, let's try this again. Slaven, imagine you are telephoning the fire brigade to report a fire. Brewer, this time you can be the fireman. "Bring, bring." That's the phone, Mr Fireman. "Bring, bring."'

'Hello.'

'Sherb's at it again.'

'Bloody hell! I'm on my way.' Laughter.

Jack Connolly is losing patience. 'Boys, all of you will need to use a telephone at some stage and you have got to be clear. When you answer the phone, begin by stating your number, and you might like to add your name. "Bring, bring." "Two-nine-one-six, Mr Connolly speaking, how can I help you?" See? Clarity. If the call is for someone else in the household, say, "Yes, I think Harold is here. I will call him." And if he's not, say, "Can I give him a message?" Understood?' There's general nodding. 'Right. Well, we might look at the telephone again tomorrow.' Then he fiddles with his pipe. 'Boys, I want each of you to write a descriptive paragraph. The subject is "An interesting view".' Then he sat down and started reading his newspaper.

Jack Connolly was dull. We could see how it would be driving Harold mad living with him. Heroin, steroids and a Volkswagen by the park in the dark would be much more preferable. Any day.

•

We started footy training after school. Brother Hugh wore his shorts, football boots and a whistle hung around his neck. We began by doing five laps of the oval to 'get us warmed up'. Then he divided us into two teams and we played touch. He refereed. Then it was ball work.

Brother Hugh liked to kick the ball. He could drop-kick really well. But mostly he'd punt the ball really high and we'd have to catch it. If you dropped it, it was a lap of the oval. Dean had poor handling and spent a lot of time doing laps. Then it was passing practice. Then it was set piece work. I worked on Mum's torpedo passing and Brother Hugh was well pleased with the combination I had going with O'Brien. O'Brien was the fastest player for his age in Lithgow. Possibly the fastest in the state. Possibly the fastest in the world.

I stayed behind and just me and Brother Hugh practised drop-kicking balls between the sticks. He had a practised routine. He'd kiss the ball before dropping it onto his foot. He didn't miss once that evening.

His other great skill was being able to hurl stones underarm. The stone went for miles. I asked him how he'd learnt to do that. He said that when he was at Oakhill College he had to stay at the school over the holidays by himself for weeks on end. He had to find things to do. Kicking footballs was one. Throwing stones was another.

He asked me if we had heard from Dad and how Mum was coping. He said he was gravely worried about Sherb.

•

Mum's typing was getting really good. She regularly topped eighty words a minute and had an interview for a job at the Small Arms Factory. She was incredibly nervous. 'Do I look like a typist?' she asked me when she emerged from the bathroom. I told her she looked like the prettiest typist in Australia. She kissed me on the forehead and headed off.

She got the job. She was now a part of the typing pool. I had never seen her this happy. It meant a better wage and much better hours. She didn't have to do the shiftwork at Berlei's anymore. She started work at eighteen minutes past seven in the morning and finished at six minutes past four in the afternoon. It was a short walk to the factory and it meant working with a few of the friends she was making at the RSL Club on Saturday nights.

We celebrated with a chicken Mum picked up at the butchery. Thankfully, Mum had a cookbook that told us how to cook it in a pot on the stove. The oven didn't work. We'd never cooked chicken before. We dined like kings while we listened to the radio. 'Requests' was on. 'Another request for Kay Green. "I'll see you behind the Showground grandstand, you are the love of my life." Kay, this has come again from Jim Keogh.' Peter and Gordon's 'Lady Godiva'. Pure Flynn, I reckoned, what with its reference to striptease.

After dinner, Mum helped me with my Maths homework and she had some good ideas for the composition Jack Connolly had given us for homework. 'A day in the life of a flat file.'

She gave Mrs Leslie her typewriter and typing textbook back and promised to make her a dress as a thankyou. Mum said it was going to use up a fair bit of material. Mrs Leslie wasn't a small woman.

•

Brother Connor has 'very exciting' news for us. 'Sit up, boys. Arms folded.' He measures us all in a bright-eyed gaze. 'We're having a retreat. Here. At the school. On Friday.' The Temperate Zone is really excited. Tropics and Tundra, less so. 'It is a wonderful opportunity for spiritual renewal. Couple of practical considerations, boys. In case the weather is inclement, make sure you have a coat of some sort, because there will be times when you will be engaging with nature. The tuckshop will be closed for the day. Lunch, ipso facto, will be provided by your good selves. Confessions will be heard for most of the morning. Father Keogh and Father Kane will be joining us for the day. Bring your missals and rosary beads. Altar boys for the mass will be Dean, Doyle, O'Brien and Flynn. Mass will be at midday. There is no possible excuse for any boy not to receive Holy Communion. A day of grace, boys.

'And you know, it often happens that boys your age get "the calling" during a retreat. There will be a sign. The sign might be just a thought, a voice, a sense of being spiritually uplifted. And when you get "the calling", it just makes so much sense. You rise, you lift, you soar! You experience direct communication with God. With God the Father, boys. You'll know it. You'll know it when it happens. It could happen to any one of you. Just keep your minds open, that's all.'

Friday was still and sunny, though the air was cool. The day started with assembly and a very poor rendition of the hymn to Saint John Baptist de La Salle. Everyone was behind the note searching for the melody. Then we went to our classrooms. Father Keogh took us. He led the saying of the Sorrowful Mysteries of the Rosary. We began with The Apostles' Creed, the Our Father, three Hail Marys, the Glory Be. Then into the five decades. It took half an hour or so.

Brother Connor takes over and leads us out of the classroom and we walk together in silence around the school oval. He sits us down near the toilets and tells us quietly that both Father Keogh and Father Kane are in the house ready to take confessions. We stand and form a queue outside the main entrance to the Brothers' quarters and present ourselves two by two.

My confession is pretty straightforward, although Father Keogh asked me whether Mum had heard from Dad and how was Mum getting on. I didn't mention Brian Lawson or the RSL Club but I told him about her new job at the Small Arms Factory. He was very pleased for her, he said, although 'there are many men about the factory, she'll want to be very careful'. I nodded, but had no idea what he was getting at.

The whole town was filled with men. What was he hoping she would do? Never go out at all? I didn't argue though. I accepted my penance.

We then clambered aboard the buses in silence and headed across town to Saint Patrick's. Mass was disappointing because there were no girls at the church. Father Kane was the celebrant. He was a bit nervous with all the Brothers and Father Keogh in the congregation. We didn't understand much of what he was saying during his sermon because he was too close to the microphone on the pulpit, and the feedback on the recently installed public address system was, at times, deafening. The worse it got, the harder he tried; and the harder he tried, the worse it got.

The buses took us back to school and it's lunchtime. It's meant to be had in silence and all staff hands are on deck for playground duty. I sit by myself on a step leading to the oval. I have two strawberry jam sandwiches Mum has made for me. They're cut into fours really nicely. They're wrapped in greaseproof paper that I have to take home with me.

I notice Dean and Doyle are whispering to each other. Benson and Brewer have stood over a terrified fifth class kid who is keeping an eye out for teachers while they have cigarettes behind the toilets, but the wafts of smoke are obvious and within ten draws Brother Connor has bailed them up and issued summary justice. They both got four on the spot. He didn't say a word. The only sound was leather on fingers. It reverberated across the otherwise silent oval. Brennan gathers some eucalyptus leaves, which he silently hands to Benson and Brewer, and they rub them vigorously between their hurting hands.

After lunchtime is meditation.

Our meditation session is supervised by Harold. We are lazing about in the afternoon sun in the north garden of the school, which is normally out of bounds. We're not allowed to speak. We are to contemplate the garden and the trees and the hills beyond and communicate with the creator of it all. And, generally speaking, we do. We try to, at least. Many of us are just lying on the lawn looking at the clouds.

Brewer is meditating on a lizard he has caught. Its feet are ensnared in his jumper. Benson has caught a fly and, lying on his stomach, is trying to get Brewer's lizard to eat it. It doesn't seem interested in the fly. Dean is asleep under a tree. Doyle and O'Brien are sitting side-by-side, against the trunks of two old camellia trees. They both look bored. I think I must look bored too, because I am. The call of a close currawong is a fleeting distraction.

Harold is seated on the lawn. He has a manila folder stuffed with material and is making corrections with a biro to some densely written pages. He turns, seeking out someone. 'Dean,' he says. 'Dean.' Dean wakes up. 'Dean, spell "Christaller" for me.'

Dean says, 'Two l's, Sir.'

'Thank you.' He scratches a correction.

Then, a minute or so passes and Flynn says, 'Dean, spell "silence" for me.'

Dean says, 'One l.'

Harold lets it go. Another minute of silence.

Brewer says, 'Dean. Spell "Lollobrigida" for me.' Sniggers aplenty.

'Boys. Enough. Lift the gaze.'

'Three l's,' says Dean. More sniggers.

Harold says, 'Uncalled for, Dean, and most unlike you, it has to be said.'

Benson chimes in, 'Dean. Spell "lust" for me.' Loud sniggers.

Harold's had it. He's quickly on his feet, standing over Benson and beating him about the head very loudly with his rolled manila folder, using both hands. It must really hurt. Benson folds himself into a ball. Harold stops. He gathers his thoughts and pushes his thick-rimmed glasses back onto his nose.

The bell rings and we gather for a parting assembly. Father Keogh leads an Our Father, and we are told by Brother Hugh, in very measured tones, to not speak until we have left the school grounds.

And there is a lot of talk. We group in clusters, bike to bike, along Amiens Street. Everyone has a story. We're as loud as a good crowd at a footy match. Some of the Temperate Zone are very excited. I overhear Mitchell and Neville saying they heard God speaking to them. Mahon says he saw a brown snake but couldn't tell anyone.

Tropics and Tundra are in a large circle. I join them. Doyle says he couldn't concentrate because of the noise of the building site. Dean complains about the new public address system at the church. Doyle reckons it was Father Kane's fault. Brewer said Father Kane was picking his nose when he had confession. Dean says when he was asleep, he dreamt of his mother tending to wounds of Jesus after he was lowered from the cross. He wonders if it might be a sign. I tell them that I heard God had spoken to Mitchell and Neville.

'Poor bastards,' says Brewer. There is laughter.

'What got into Harold?' asks O'Brien.

We hang around for about half an hour. The crowd dwindles. Then it's just us. Benson's hands are causing him difficulty. He thinks he's getting arthritis 'or something'. He can't grip the handlebars of his bike. He's a bit distressed. Dean looks at his hands. We all do. All his fingers are swollen and bruised. Two fingers are black. Dean asks him how many cuts he's had this week. Flynn knew precisely. 'Twenty-four.'

There had been some concern about Benson for a while now. For some reason, he was almost deliberately getting up the noses of all teachers. I had overheard Dean and Doyle talking about it. Doyle assumed something must be going on at home. Dean agreed.

Dean takes charge. Dean will double Benson home, which is well out of his way. Benson lived at Oaky Park. Brewer, instead of taking the bus, is instructed to take Benson's bike for safekeeping.

Dean, being Dean, went one step further. He doubled Benson to the hospital, all the way up the steepest hill in Lithgow, and sought his mum. His mum looked at Benson's hands and treated him immediately. And Mr Dean and Mrs Dean were at the school that night asking how it could be possible that a boy could be struck across the hands so often. It was cruel, bordering on criminal. Brother Connor was given a severe dressing-down by the Deans and by Brother Hugh. It was the best thing to come out of the retreat.

Chapter Eleven

'Doyle, Doyle, Doyle, why don't I believe you?'
BROTHER CONNOR

'All the way with LBJ.'
HAROLD HOLT, PRIME MINISTER OF AUSTRALIA

I'm back at Doyle's on Saturday night. He said if it was a clear night we might be able to see Saturn. I arrive at half past eight and he's in the backyard standing by a white telescope mounted on a timber tripod. The telescope is about three feet long with the eyepiece at forty-five degrees to the barrel. It takes him a while to line up what he's looking for and, when he does, he invites me to have a look.

I see Saturn. I can see two thick rings around it. It's small, but really clear. It just hangs there. It is beautiful. After a minute it disappears from view and he adjusts the direction of the telescope to find it again. Then he finds Jupiter and we can see a line of moons surrounding it. While I watch, he disappears and comes back with a bottle of Cottee's Passiona for me. Then he finds what he calls a nebula. 'Orion's Nebula,' he tells me. 'It's where stars are being formed. What we're seeing is happening years in the past, it takes light that amount of time to reach us.' I can't wait to tell Mum. Then he shows me one of the Southern Cross pointers. 'Beta Centauri is actually two stars. Alpha Centauri is around four light years away.' He explains how distance is measured by time.

'Could we show Mum, sometime?'

'Yeah,' he says.

Then his grandma is at the back door. 'John, have you done the milk crates?'

'Yes, Ma.'

'What are you doing out there?'

'Looking at the planets, Ma.'

'What nonsense.'

'It's all nonsense, Ma. Everything is.'

She's not interested in taking the conversation any further and heads off to her quarters. Her flat at the back of the house has its own kitchen and everything. She turns the lights on in her rooms and the light spills out from her windows into the yard, making any further viewing impossible. We go inside. He packs the telescope away into a long red box that sits in the beer room behind some cartons of DA.

We settle on the floor of the beer room. We talk about the retreat. Doyle speculates as to who might have received 'the calling'. He reckons Dean would be the most likely. I can see what he means. Dean is without doubt the most sensible among us. We then get talking about what sort of priest Benson would be and what sort of kid Brother Connor would have been.

From the kitchen comes a blood-curdling scream. Doyle flies into the kitchen.

When I arrive, Jen is bent over, holding her stomach. She has the bone of a cooked lamb chop in her hand. Other bones are strewn around the floor. The fridge door is open. She is groaning. 'I'm going to be sick. I'm going to be sick!'

Doyle steers her towards the toilet beside the beer room. 'Come on, mate.'

She is wailing in agony.

The door to Grandma's rooms opens. She shouts, 'Are you there, John?'

He opens the toilet door. 'She found the chops, Ma. I forgot to tie the fridge.'

Grandma stands in the doorway.

The moaning becomes a loud projectile vomit, most of which goes into the toilet. 'Oh, God! God! God!' Jen shouts.

Now Cath is up. She is tired. She looks at what is going on, turns and returns to bed.

Doyle is wiping Jen's face with a damp washer. 'How's your tummy now, mate?'

'Oh, what has she done, now,' she says in someone else's voice. 'She can't be trusted. She's been at the fridge.'

'Okay, mate, back to bed.'

She's happy to go.

The door to Grandma's rooms closes. Doyle takes Jen to her room. When he returns, he picks up the bones from the kitchen floor and puts them in the rubbish bin under the sink. He buckles the thick belt around the fridge door, before attacking the toilet with a mop and bucket.

We sit in the lounge room. 'She has to be supervised. She doesn't chew her food. It's got to be cut up for her. I'm lucky she didn't swallow the bones. For years I prayed to God that He might intervene. Make her normal, God. Please. Please, just make her normal. Miraculously, she wakes up one morning and is normal. And then I pray that she's taken in her sleep. She just doesn't wake up. She just goes to Heaven. Take her home to you, Jesus. And I think maybe I should take matters into my own hands and put a pillow over her face and she suffocates very quickly and she's in Heaven and we can . . .' He shrugs. 'Sometimes, I think I hate her. And when I do, I hate myself. But I don't hate her. Not at all. It's not her fault. I just hate the circumstance.'

I can't think of anything to say.

Doyle goes on. 'What sort of God does that to a girl? Eh? What sort of God gives a girl a life of confusion and misery? What sort of God makes a girl want to smash her own face in? What sort of God invents autism? Or polio? Or cancer? "These things are sent to try us. We live in a vale of tears. We're somehow blessed to have such a cross to bear." Bullshit. There are only two answers. Either there is no God. Or God is a cunt.'

I say nothing.

Then he says, 'It'll be a whole rosary for penance this week. Again.'

We go outside and in the cold air look at the stars. The moon is rising. Doyle lights a Benson & Hedges. I ride off into the night, both unnerved and excited by Doyle's insights into Heaven and the heavens.

•

The fire is well underway when Mum gets in. She is furious. Brian Lawson has ruined her night. 'Roy, he wouldn't leave me alone. Insisted on buying me drinks. Pulled his chair over and joined our table. Just barged in. Talked about himself when we're trying to listen to the band. Kathy Wilson says he's the most boring man in Australia and I said that's what I said last week. I had to put my foot down when he was pleading to take me home. Eventually Brandt's dad, Ally, helps me out. Brandt plays in the band, good guitarist. His father's a bit of a thug. Scares people a bit. He pushed Brian in the chest in the car park. He lost his footing and fell over. I left them to it and ducked into Kathy's car. Now I'm worried he might have got beaten up or something and it's somehow my fault. I can't go back to the RSL Club. And I've made good friends there. I love it there. I don't know what to do.'

Mum looks at me. 'What have you been up to?'

'Went to Doyle's. He's got a telescope. We saw the rings of Saturn and the moons of Jupiter. Mum, it's incredible. I'd love you to see it.'

'Could he bring it around here, sometime?'

'Yeah, I suppose.'

It was predictable that the black Zephyr would appear out the front of the house Sunday afternoon. I saw it through the window. 'Mum! Brian's here.'

She turns the radio off. And the lights. 'We're not home,' she whispers. We sit on the floor. There's a knock at the door. We freeze. The knock is repeated. We can hear him walking along the front verandah. Now his head's against the window. Eventually he walks off.

I poke my head up.

'Don't let him see you,' Mum whispers.

'I can't see him,' I say.

Mum panics. 'Roy! Make sure the back door is locked.'

I scurry through to the back door and slip the bolt. Then there's knocking at the back door. The door handle is turned. Then I hear him move away.

I'm back on the floor with Mum. Again I poke my head up and peer through the window. I watch him get back into his car. 'Mum, he's going. And he's got a black eye.' The Zephyr moves off.

Mum breathes a sigh of relief. 'Oh, God, he'll be back.' She looks at me. 'We might have to leave town.'

And I know she's joking. I hope she's joking. Life's actually been pretty good since Dad left.

We keep the lights off for a good twenty minutes. I keep

an eye on the street through the window. It's starting to get dark. 'Where does Brian live?'

'Cupro Street.'

It's not far away. 'Keep the lights off 'til I get back. I'll make sure he's home.'

'Oh, that's silly. You don't have to do that, love.'

I head off. It's a ten-minute ride. I spot his car. It's under a carport. I approach the front door. Knock. He answers. 'Oh, hello, Tiger.'

'Brian, Mum thought you should know that Dad's come home.'

'Oh. Oh, dear me.'

'See you.' I head off.

'Thanks, Tiger!' he shouts.

•

I told Doyle what I'd done. He said it was a mortal sin. 'You have broken a commandment. "Thou shalt not bear false witness against thy neighbour." And now you've compromised me. I have a duty now to tell poor old Brian that he's been deceived, and to tell your mum that you have been making up stories about her. And if I don't do these things, I'm in sin as well. Are you happy to have me go to Hell?' I didn't know if he was serious or not.

Then he said, 'Why don't we write Brian a letter. From your father, saying that he's going to kill him if he ever sees him dribbling around your mum? Let's get stuck in.'

A few days later, Doyle was looking for dog turds in Queen Elizabeth Park. He had asked me to help. I did the spotting and he pushed the turds into a brown paper bag with the aid of a stick. I don't know what he's doing but the turds are really fresh. They stink.

That night we meet outside Brian's house. The car is there. Doyle slips up to the front door, puts the brown paper bag on the door mat, sets fire to it and rings the doorbell. I hadn't seen the doorbell when I called in. We ride away at speed.

We pull up outside Coates Hardware Store on Main Street. Doyle explains what would have happened. 'Brian's opened the door, seen the fire and stamped it out with his feet. He's then walked dog shit through his house.' Job done. We laugh and say goodnight.

On my ride home I wondered whether Brian deserved such treatment. I felt a bit sorry for him. If he really likes Mum, he can't be all bad. I felt a bit guilty. Doyle said he had some other plans for Brian. I realised that Brother Connor was probably right, Doyle could take things too far.

•

It's Saturday. Nine thirty in the morning. I am resting on my bike beside Doyle, Dean, Flynn, Brewer and O'Brien. A bike cluster of Publics is beside us led by Hammond, Beasley and Pitt. They were all decent law-abiding Publics. There would be no scuffles or fighting. We are looking at the showroom of Hassans Walls Motors, the Holden dealership in Main Street.

The showroom is curtained and the curtain is about to open to reveal the new HR Holden. We had only seen an 'artist's impression' in *The Mercury*.

The curtains part. The new Holden is magnificent. Three models are on the showroom floor – the Premier, the Special and the Standard. They are arranged perfectly. The colours, the trim, everything gets enthusiastic nods of approval. Brewer says it shits all over the Falcon. The Publics are just as enthusiastic. We nod approvals to each other. We put our bikes down together and walk into the showroom to get up close. Dean is in the lead. He opens the driver's door of the Premier. We poke our heads in. The new car smell is irresistible. We all want to sit in the driver's seat. A salesman called Les bears down on us. 'What do you lot think you're doing? Bugger off. You can't touch the cars. Bugger off.'

We go back out to our bikes. Flynn points out the Publics have been allowed to stay in the showroom. Through the window we watch Les open the bonnet and show the Publics the engine of the Premier. Brewer calls Les a prick. We all think he is.

We're at a bit of a loose end. Dean says we should climb Scotsman's Hill. It was a cool day, but sunny. Not much wind. We agree to meet at the base of the hill. Flynn hatches a plan. 'Let's meet at one o'clock, do the hill and look at the netball when we come down.' The girls played competitive netball on Saturday afternoons. It seemed a good plan. A Flynn plan. Girls were involved.

The climb goes pretty well. It's a well-worn track. Brennan has joined us. It takes us about twenty-five minutes of fully focused climbing to arrive at the summit, and we sit and look down over the town. We're breathing heavily. We can see right across the neck of the valley to Hassans Walls. We can see all but Flynn and O'Brien's houses. We can see the netballers gathering below us. About twenty cars have arrived. We can see the smoke from a soundless train arriving from Sydney. Some of the chimneys of the homes are putting out a soft grey smoke, which converges and sits over the valley like a gentle warming blanket. Brewer says he thinks it's possibly the best view in the world. Dean argues the Three Sisters is pretty good. But, as Brewer points out, you can't see Lithgow from the Three Sisters. Flynn thinks the Scotsman's Hill view shits all over the Three Sisters.

Doyle says the best view he's ever seen is at Killcare Heights on the Central Coast. 'You look south down the coastline to Lion Island and Palm Beach.'

Brewer says he hates the coast. 'I hate the beach. We went to The Entrance last year. Dad says never again.'

Brennan can't understand why anyone would want to go away for holidays. 'Mate. Everything is here. I'm never going anywhere. Dad says being home is a holiday.'

Dean says he's been to West Wyalong.

'What's it like?'

Dean says, 'Flat.'

Flynn says Cowra is shithouse. 'Worse than Forbes.'

Brennan says Wellington is shithouse, Orange is shithouse and Mudgee is really shithouse. O'Brien says he hates Bathurst. Doyle says he has a sister in Bathurst. 'She reckons the tennis courts are as good as ours.' Brewer says he'd never go to Bathurst just to play tennis. None of us would.

We all agreed that to be born and raised in Lithgow gave us a huge advantage in life.

Then the talk turns to 'dicks', 'pricks', 'deadshits' and 'arseholes'.

Jack Connolly?

'Dick,' says Brennan.

'Deadshit,' says Brewer.

Doyle agrees with Brewer. 'Jack is definitely a deadshit. Harold thinks he's a deadshit.'

'What about Harold?'

Brewer thinks. 'Bit of a prick.' There is no disagreement.

'Brother Hugh?'

'Deadshit.'

'Father Kane?'

'Deadshit.'

'Father Keogh?'

'Deadshit.'

'Les, at Hassans Walls Motors?'

'Arsehole.'

'Father Grannal?'

Brennan thinks Grannal is okay. There is no argument.

'Sherb?'

Dean says Sherb's just a bit mad, but his heart's in the right place. We agree.

'Brother Connor?'

A chorus of 'Arsehole'.

Doyle, Flynn, Brennan and O'Brien light up Benson & Hedges, provided by Doyle. Dean and I wander towards the Wallaby Rocks. Dean's interested in the rock formations. I spot a bird's nest, but no birds. Dean's not that interested in the nest. He seems to only have eyes for the rocks. Eventually the smokers join us and Doyle finds some conglomerate rock and he and Dean point out the seashells in the stone.

'At some stage all of this was part of the sea floor,' says Doyle. Brewer is sceptical. His scepticism is ignored. Dean and Doyle have found some deep fissures in the rocks. Dean drops a stone down one and Doyle counts the number of seconds it takes to clatter to the bottom. Nine seconds. They work out, allowing for friction, that the fissure is about three hundred yards deep. Brennan reckons a heavier rock would get to the bottom faster. Dean and Doyle disagree. Doyle remembers Brother Michael telling us that Galileo had proven Brennan wrong when he dropped spheres of different weights from the Leaning Tower of Pisa. 'They hit the ground at the same time.'

Brennan thinks Galileo was a 'deadshit'.

'Prick, I hear,' says Flynn.

'And an arsehole,' Brewer adds.

Doyle says, 'Well, a smartarse, for sure.'

We spend ten minutes looking for fossils. Or rather, we watch Dean, Doyle and Flynn look for fossils. They don't find anything.

A red kangaroo bounds by. Brewer reckons if Sherb was with us it would have jumped on his head. We laugh at being reminded of the goanna. Brennan's sorry he missed it. But he can picture it.

We scramble back down Scotsman's Hill and it's just a stone's throw to the netball courts. We ride over and there's quite a few blokes watching. Many of the girls have boyfriends with cars. We shout out a bit of encouragement to the team from Saint Pat's, which includes Barbara and Deirdre from the pool. Margot is the captain and she's a really good player. Marilyn is there as well. She'd been really sick earlier in the year, O'Brien points out. Marilyn lives in Doyle's street.

A carload of Slaters arrives, and the mood changes. They start heckling the girls. 'Give us a root, mole,' one of them yells. 'Come on, mole!'

To Dean it's unclear which girl is being referred to. It becomes clear when one of the Public girls, Flynn said her name was Lorraine, approaches the Slater car and screams, 'Why don't you just fuck off, Gary!' Some car horns toot and there are calls from cars, 'Yeah, Gary, fuck off.'

Gary doesn't seem to want to fuck off. He gets out of the car and gets into a slanging match with Lorraine. The game has stopped. He follows her onto the netball court.

'Don't you ever tell me to fuck off!'

'I'm telling you to fuck off now.'

A teammate shouts, 'Leave her alone, Gary.'

'Shut up, slut,' he barks back.

Car horns blare. Gary approaches Lorraine and grabs her by the shoulder. She spins around and smacks him across the face with full force. He shapes to throw a punch but has second thoughts. 'You'll keep, bitch.' He storms off, walks right past us. Looks at Dean. 'What are you looking at, cunt?' He takes a few steps, stops and turns to us. 'I hate fuck'n Tykes!' He gets back into the Ford Falcon, the engine roars, and after an elaborate burning of rubber and a doughnut, the Slaters hare off. The game recommences.

Doyle says there are times when language is inadequate.

O'Brien says, 'Oh, I don't know, cunt isn't bad.' There is general agreement.

Doyle says, 'Well, it's all we've got.'

Brennan shakes his head. 'Fuck'n Publics.'

Chapter Twelve

'Let your chief study be the Bible, that it
may be the guiding rule of your life.'
SAINT JOHN BAPTIST

'Music is the soundtrack of your life.'
DICK CLARK

That Saturday night I go around to Brewer's to watch television. We watch a film called *The Informers*. It's pretty dull. The best thing about it is the ads. Mrs Brewer had made a chocolate cake, which was really nice.

Mrs Brewer looks at me. 'Well?' she says. 'What's it like with Dad back?'

I say, 'Dad's not back, Mrs Brewer.'

'Oh. I was told he was. Someone down the street told me. Mrs Dougherty. He's not back?'

'No.'

She seems disappointed.

She wanted to know whether Mum was enjoying working at the Small Arms Factory. 'I know they work very hard in the typing pool.'

'She's really enjoying it, Mrs Brewer.'

'I'm so pleased. Is she at the RSL Club again, tonight?'

'Yeah. She likes the band there.'

'That's Tony Doyle's band, isn't it?'

'That's right.'

'Is Tom Doyle still playing, Jack?'

Mr Brewer thought he was.

'He's a good sax player, Tom Doyle. He played at the Catholic Ball last year, didn't he, Jack?'

'Yes. Yes, he did.'

'All the Doyles play instruments. Or sing. Or both. John's in your class, does he play an instrument?' I tell her he's playing at the bowling club with his Uncle Ray tonight. Bass guitar.

'At his age? In the clubs? It's not right.'

•

I've got the fire blazing nicely when Mum gets in. She has had the greatest night in the history of greatest nights. No sign of Brian Lawson. 'I couldn't believe it. It made such a difference. Kathy's friends are theatre people. Des Davies runs the show. He was there tonight. Knows so much, that man. He's asked me if I'd like to go to an acting class. Thursday night. And you know what, Roy? I just might go. Do you mind?'

I didn't mind at all. I told her how good Mrs Brewer's chocolate cake had been. Mum said she wouldn't have the first idea as to how to make a chocolate cake. Nor was she interested in learning.

•

Mum's week was sort of taken up with what to wear to the acting class. She decided on slacks and a skivvy and flatties. Then she threw a scarf around her neck and said, 'What do you think?' I told her she looked like Elizabeth Taylor. And she did a bit.

•

Brother Hugh had organised a footy match against a school from Springwood. A public high school. We played at the Glanmire. They were a pretty good team. They were older than us. They had a really good centre called Graham Eadie who gave us all sorts of trouble and at half-time we were down fifteen to five. He was big, fast and elusive and he read the game really well.

Brother Hugh spoke with us during the break and said we had to mark Eadie closely and to tackle him 'on suspicion'. I said that I could read him pretty well and suggested I play centre in defence and stay at five-eighth in attack. Brother Hugh agreed.

The plan worked really well. Eadie did nothing in the second half, I could see clearly when they were going to pass the ball to him and hit him as he received it, every time. He really got the shits with me. Wanted to go on with it. Twice. Earned us two penalties.

We had enough ball for me to set up O'Brien with three tries in the second half. Two came from kicks and the third from a pass I threw into the gap and O'Brien sailed onto it, wrong-footing Eadie, who was really angry. He remonstrated with the ref. 'That pass was miles forward!' The ref, Mr Hammond, waved him away. Flynn kicked well to convert the tries and we won the game eighteen to fifteen. Brother Hugh was the proudest man on the planet. He was especially proud of Dean and Marsland who had matched it with their older opposition forwards.

There was only one moment of nastiness. A scrum had broken up and the Springwood halfback threw a punch at Dean, who was in the front row. It collected him flush on the jaw. We got a penalty but Dean was most aggrieved. Later, I lined up the halfback, who was a yappy, busy player, and grabbed him and held him up on his feet long enough for Dean to put his shoulder into the bloke's ribs. He was winded. Dean winked at me in appreciation.

•

The school social was bearing down on us. It was to be held at the Saint Patrick's school hall and Brother Connor emphasised that attendance was 'mandatory'. He spoke a lot about 'etiquette'.

'We don't get many opportunities to engage with the fairer sex, boys, but there are do's and don'ts. When approaching a young lady for a dance, you will say something along the lines of, "Excuse me, Miss, but would you do me the honour of accompanying me to the dance floor?" She will say something like, "It would be a pleasure, Sir." You then extend your hand and she will take it and you both proceed to the dance floor.

'Then there is the issue of small talk. You ask yourself what might this young lady be interested in talking about? Now. Benson, what might a young lady be interested in talking about?'

Benson considered. 'She might be interested in cars, Brother.'

'Cars, Benson?'

Brother Connor liked this. He looked away from the window and fixed Benson in his eye. 'Benson, imagine I am the young lady you have approached. Let's see how this conversation might play out. You can address me as . . . Maureen.' Brother Connor sat at his desk. 'Well? Come on, Benson, on your feet, Maureen is waiting.'

Benson stood and approached the front desk. Brother Connor looked at him and smiled.

'Excuse me, Maureen, can I have a dance with you?'

Brother Connor stood and extended his hand. 'You may,' he said.

'What sort of car do you like, Maureen?'

'Any car that gets me safely where I want to go.'

Benson was a bit flummoxed. 'I like Holdens.'

'Sit down, Benson. Maureen is bored. Can any of you think of a better subject that might appeal to Maureen?'

Dean put his hand up.

'Dean?'

'Television shows, Brother.'

'Good. Yes. Anyone else? Yes, Brewer?'

'Flowers, Brother. Maureen might like talking about flowers.'

'Good. Maybe. Doyle?'

'Teachers. Favourite teachers, Brother.'

Brother Connor nodded. 'Well, Doyle, let's see how this plays out. Maureen is ready.'

Doyle stands and approaches the front desk. 'Excuse me, Maureen, I was hoping to have the pleasure of your company for the next dance.'

'Certainly, Sir.'

'We are blessed, Maureen, with the most wonderful teachers. My favourite is Brother Connor. Who might your favourite be?'

'Oh, and why do you like this Brother Connor so much?'

'Because he reminds me of you, Maureen.'

This exchange garners some giggles.

Brother Connor thinks. 'Sit down, thank you, Doyle. While I'm a little troubled as to where this conversation might be heading, at least it's in an open direction. And that's the point. Show an interest in the girl. Try to learn something about her. Tell her how nice she looks, even if she doesn't. Now. I want you to place your hands on the desk. I'm looking at your nails, boys.'

He wandered along each row examining our hands. 'Putrid, Flynn. Ditto, Brewer. Appalling, Brennan. Benson, I hate to imagine what might lie beneath those rags. Boys, I will be checking all your fingernails tomorrow. Make sure they pass muster.'

Most hands 'passed muster' the next day and, among ourselves, we referred to Brother Connor as 'Maureen' for the rest of the year.

While Mum readied herself for her drama class, I prepared for the social. I only had one jacket to wear, a sort of grey check that used to be Dad's. It fitted okay. Mum let me wear my good green corduroy jeans and, with a green shirt and red tie and my polished school shoes, Mum said I would win some hearts. She was pretty nervous about the drama class with Mr Davies.

Mum trimmed my hair and fashioned it in a sort of Beatles style and I felt reasonably confident of not being a total embarrassment.

It was a cool night. Mr Dean and Mr Goggin were on the door. The hall had chairs set all around the perimeter, with a long table at one end brimming with bottles of warm soft drink that could be purchased. Sister Valerian manned the table. Everyone was standing around, the boys up one end and the girls down the other.

I quickly joined a circle that included Flynn, O'Brien, Brewer, Dean, Benson, Doyle and Brennan. Benson wore his school uniform, which marked him out as a real loser. He was the only one to have to do so. He had no good clothes. We said nothing about it, but were aware of how self-conscious he felt. It wasn't helped when Maureen breezed by, saying, 'My, oh my, Benson, you shouldn't have gone to so much trouble.' What he missed was that Benson had new white dressings on his hands, courtesy of Dean and his mum, no doubt.

Benson had, for some reason or other, earned the reputation of being a behaviour problem. He managed to annoy just about all the teachers with the exception of Sherb. Sherb had a soft spot for him. We assumed it was because Benson always had smokes on him and Sherb had taken to botting the odd fag. He had a jockey's build, permanent dandruff and a series of scabs that appeared to move about his face. When nervous, he picked at these scabs, and he was nervous a lot. His behaviour, at worst, was cheeky. He looked cheeky all the time. He couldn't help it.

We saw him rarely outside of school. He was never at the pool. He seemed to spend a lot of his time near and around the greyhound track, although he was never actually seen with a dog. He had difficulty telling right from left, so that his b's and d's were an inconsistent lottery in any word, or worb. He was, therefore, a very soft target for teachers who enjoyed bullying, like Brother Connor. I think Benson just wanted to be left alone. He wasn't a serious behaviour problem; he just had problems.

Brother Hugh looked very angry. It seemed Sister Geraldine had had some words with him. It looked like it was going to be her show, not his, because she took to the microphone on stage to welcome us all. He stood down the back of the hall and seethed. Without the role of MC, he was largely irrelevant.

The music was provided by Mrs Dougherty on piano, Roger Willis on drums and Sister Francis with her acoustic guitar. To say the music was woeful was to be kind.

Sister Geraldine then asked the boys to choose their partners for the Canadian Three Step. I asked Barbara and she agreed. Barbara had heard the disagreement between the co-principals. Sister Geraldine had done all the talking and Brother Hugh had sort of spluttered some incoherent noises. I told her I knew the noises she was talking about.

We negotiated the dance reasonably well, Barbara reminding me of the steps. At its conclusion, I escorted her back to her chair and thanked her. Flynn had danced with Deirdre, and O'Brien with Marilyn. Dean had danced with one of the Cullen girls. Doyle had danced with Carmel, and Benson had sat it out. I missed seeing Brennan or Brewer dancing.

I asked Barbara for a dance four times. I was really enjoying her company and she was starting to relax with me. We both took time to observe Brother Hugh and enjoyed sharing our observations.

'Did you see him with Sister Valerian?'

I hadn't.

'She offered him a bottle of drink.'

'What happened? He went the colour of beetroot?'

She laughed. 'And dropped the bottle.'

I laughed.

At what was deemed half-time, we were, in Sister Geraldine's words, to be given a special treat. Father Keogh had agreed to sing for us. He strode onto the stage. A white handkerchief held in his left hand, he placed his right on the top of the piano and struck what I took to be a singer's pose. Roger Willis and Sister Francis weren't needed. He opened with 'When Irish Eyes Are Smiling' in a sort of reedy tenor voice, before segueing seamlessly into 'Too-Ra-Loo-Ra-Loo-Ral' where he really gained in confidence. The main problem was that it was difficult to watch. With each note sung, foam gathered about his mouth and no one really wanted to follow where it might end up. But we were all somehow compelled to follow it. There was a palpable sense of relief when the handkerchief came into play, scooping up what looked to be a plasma snowball that could have had a mind of its own if unchecked.

The applause was for the scooping, rather than the singing, but he misread the room and launched into 'Danny Boy' in a key Mrs Dougherty had quite a bit of difficulty finding on the piano keyboard. And he doggedly stuck to his key despite Mrs Dougherty's many chordal suggestions. His key remained between the white notes and the black notes throughout. Doyle said that it was a very hard thing to do, requiring a complete and total absence of listening skills. Mercifully 'Danny Boy' came to its discordant conclusion. There was desultory applause and the dancing could recommence.

The Progressive Barn Dance was sort of interesting. Sister Valerian grabbed Benson by the arm and marched him across to one of the Second Form girls and together they both unwillingly participated. Many girls presented with a scrunched handkerchief in hand, and often it was damp with what could only be a perfumed mucus. And there were height issues. Some of the girls were tiny and embarrassed when lifted into the air. At the call of 'Ladies' Choice', many blokes bought bottles of soft drink and therefore had excuses not to be asked. Barbara asked me and we negotiated the Pride of Erin with her very much in the lead.

The night finished off with the Hokey-Pokey, which the teachers loved but the rest of us hated, apart from a few simpletons from Second Form. Then there were lots of parents gathered around the door ready to take their adolescents home.

A carload of Slaters arrived looking for stragglers to monster. They wound down the windows of the Falcon and shouted at some of the girls. 'Tyke mole' was a recurring reference. That, and 'What are you looking at?' and 'You'll go, four eyes.' The last directed at Mr Goggin, who threatened to call the police.

Mr Doyle was waiting for Doyle. He asked me if I wanted a lift home, as being bailed up by a Slater was a real possibility. I grabbed the opportunity. Walking meant taking back streets.

On our way to the Doyle Valiant, we noticed Benson scurrying off. 'Can we give Benson a lift, Dad?'

Mr Doyle was happy to do it, so Benson was given the offer, which he grabbed with both bandaged hands. Doyle and his father talked about the band on the way to Oaky Park, where Benson lived.

'Great band tonight, Dad, you'd have liked it.'

'I heard most of the last bracket. The guitar made it very modern, didn't it?'

'I suppose it did, Dad. Yeah. Modern. Modern is the word.'

Mr Doyle was apparently just as sarcastic as Doyle.

Benson directs us to his house. There is no street lighting. The house turns out to be a caravan with a corrugated-iron lean-to attached to the side. 'Thanks, Mr Doyle,' and Benson disappeared into the darkness.

On the way to my place, Mr Doyle sings 'Ticket To Ride'. Then he asks, 'Why Ryde? Why is she going to Ryde?'

Doyle doesn't respond. I think he's heard it before.

I say, 'She might have fallen in love with someone who lives in Ryde.'

Mr Doyle says, 'Sure. A swarthy bloke, with too much grease in his hair. She's not going to be happy.'

Doyle says, 'We're in trouble with our haircuts, Dad. The Bab is having a crackdown on what he calls "square cuts". As of tonight, they're illegal. He's mad, Dad.'

Brother Hugh had become 'the Bab' after his 'What do you take me for? A baboon?' had become a bit of a mantra.

Mr Doyle nods. Mr Doyle has been Doyle's barber for years. Doyle's grandmother took him to Stan Kuzmac's in town in First Form and the result was Doyle's mother declaring, 'Never again.'

I get dropped off. My worst fear is realised. The black Zephyr is parked outside the house. I enter from the back lane, hoping to be able to get to my room unnoticed. Mum calls, 'We're in here, Roy,' in a voice I don't recognise.

The fire is lit. It must have been Brian's doing. Mum has nothing to do with the fire. Brian has a big grin on his face. 'Here he is. The boy who makes up stories. And I don't blame you for that. Not at all. Not in the least. I put myself in your position and I would do the same. You were protecting your mother from a perceived threat. But I am not a threat. And Paulette agrees that I am not a threat. But what I am more concerned about is the bill for fourteen dollars to have my home fumigated and cleaned.'

With a theatrical flourish, he produces the bill from his coat pocket and places it on the table. 'Well?' Mum speaks. 'Did you do it, Roy?'

'Do what?'

'Place faeces on my doorstep and set fire to it!'

'No, I didn't. I tell you who has been doing that sort of stuff, Gary Slater.'

Mum says, 'Oh, they're bad, the Slaters.' She picks the bill up off the table and looks me in the eye. 'God's honour, Roy? God's honour?'

'God's honour, Mum, it was not me.'

She hands the bill back to Brian. 'I know my son, Brian. He did not do it.'

Brian looks at me with unvarnished loathing. 'You haven't heard the last on this matter, Paulette, I'm sorry to say.' He heads for the front door. 'I'll let myself out.'

Mum and I walk towards the lounge room window and see the cabin of his car light up. The Zephyr takes off. We hold the moment.

Mum turns to me and gives me a warm hug. 'You're my hero, Roy. My hero.' She kisses me on the forehead.

'It was Doyle, Mum. Doyle did it.'

'What?'

'He was trying to help.'

Mum wants all the details. When I give them to her she says, 'Oh, that's shocking. I've never heard of . . .' And she laughs. 'No, that's really, really, shocking. It's not funny.' She looks at me. 'I think this Doyle is dangerous. He might be bad company. He is Tony Doyle's brother, isn't he?' She thinks. 'Of course he is. I knew that. I don't know, Roy. I don't want you getting into trouble.'

She loved the acting class. 'It was . . .' She couldn't find a word that possessed enough excellence and wonder. There is talk of a production of a musical called *The Boy Friend*. She thinks she might audition. Mum and I talk until after two in the morning. I give her all the details of the social and she tells me all about her new drama friends. She started to talk about Dad but thought better of it. It was the latest I had ever been to bed.

Chapter Thirteen

'Some students require great mildness, while
others need to be directed with firmness.'
SAINT JOHN BAPTIST

'Sit down, Marsland, you big, hairy galoot.'
BROTHER HUGH CORCORAN

I thought I should break the ice between Mum and Doyle, so at lunchtime I asked him if he would come around with his telescope. He looked at the sky for clouds. He asked Dean what the cloud number was.

Dean and Doyle run the weather station, which was a large white slatted box in the school's north garden. The school gets a bit of money from the Bureau of Meteorology for the work. I've been with Doyle when he's done it during the holidays. There's a wet bowl and a dry bowl and a thermometer and a barometer, and measurements are taken and encoded into a green book. Cloud coverage is assessed with each cloud type given a percentage. The coded numbers are relayed over the Brothers' telephone to the bureau. This is done twice a day at nine in the morning and three in the afternoon. It only became possible when the school got a telephone. Doyle and Dean each have a key to the Brothers' house.

Crawlers. They get rewards.

Dean says, 'Four.'

Doyle nods and says, 'Why not tonight?'

He walked over that night, carrying the red box that housed the telescope. He arrived with a brown paper bag filled with chocolate biscuits, including four chocolate marshmallows. All Arnott's. It was a good start. Mum asked him how his sister was.

'She's not much fun, Mrs Slaven. But Mum and Doctor Leslie are working on changing her tablets.'

'What's it called? The thing she's got? Roy told me, but I can't . . .'

'Autism.'

'And what is that precisely?'

'I don't know. She's somehow trapped. Trapped inside herself. She can read and write. Hates it. She can't focus on anything. Well, she can, but it's nothing she can share. She makes little star-like shapes from the silver paper she pulls out of Mum's cigarette packets and will twist them in her fingers, watching the light sparkle and refract. She does this for hours. She keeps them. She has thousands of them. She calls them her "twiddlies". She rocks on the lounge, on the floor, on her bed, for hours. She will fixate on a word or a phrase, for hours. She has the loudest voice in Australia. She screams and screams, for hours. And she is at war with her own face. And she must be supervised at all times. She's not much fun, Mrs Slaven.'

Mum shakes her head.

'They go to the Workies, don't they? Your parents?'

'Saturday nights, yes. Mum and Dad have one night out a week. Otherwise, they would go mad. Mum might be a bit mad already. We have her mum living with us now. Ma. And she's not much fun either. Sometimes she winds Jen up. She imagines harsh discipline will correct her behaviour. She makes her write with her right hand. Jen's left-handed. Ma's wrong. She's wrong about a lot of things.'

Mum rugs up and we head outside. The clouds come and go. Doyle sets up the telescope beside the coal heap. He tries to set up too quickly and it takes him longer. He's nervous with Mum watching. Don't often see Doyle nervous, unless it's facing the opening ball from Ronnie Horner.

He gets the tripod stable and lines up the telescope. He finds Saturn. But Mum bumps it when placing her feet between lumps of coal and the legs of the tripod. We have to start again. Mum thinks we should get a torch. She starts to get a bit impatient. He's found it again and Mum is extra careful.

'Just let the image settle on your eye,' he says.

It does. Mum squeals. She looks again. 'It's moving.'

'Yeah. You have to follow it.'

'Saturn. My god. It's beautiful, John. Beautiful. I am so impressed.'

John Doyle

The clouds are thickening so we call it a day. It's really cold. We go inside and Mum hugs the fire while the jug boils.

'How'd you get on with Maureen's homework?'

I said I hadn't done it yet.

Mum asks who Maureen is.

'Brother Connor,' we say in unison.

Doyle tells her the story. He impersonates Brother Connor with Benson. It's really good. Mum is astonished.

'Is any of this true, Roy?'

'Exactly as it was, Mum.'

'He's sick, isn't he? Honestly, those Brothers, they're all mad.' She shakes her head. Doyle said he was working with Doctor Leslie on changing Maureen's medication. Mum laughed.

When Doyle left, Mum stood by the fire in thought. 'He's not dangerous. He's different to Tony, though. Tony's a funny man. A real entertainer. John's . . . darker. But he's not dangerous. He is a good friend for you.'

I didn't tell her about his pretending to be a 2LT announcer with the telephone with Mrs Abbott. I did Maureen's homework.

•

It's Thursday, last period. Jack Connolly is talking about how writing an essay is very similar to building a coffee table. While he teaches, Dean and Doyle are doing their Maths homework. The Temperate Zone is drinking in his words. The Tundra is looking for trouble. Benson has worked up a stiffy and is showing it to Brewer. Brewer gets Brennan to have a look at it.

176

They start giggling. Jack Connolly stops speaking mid-sentence. The room is suddenly very still. The Bab is standing at the back of the classroom. He is red in the face. He is not happy. He walks up an aisle, stopping beside Benson. Through tight lips he says, 'Put it away, Benson. Put it away.' He then looks at the back of each of our heads. He asks some to stand.

Standing are Brewer, Flynn, O'Brien, Dean, Doyle, Brennan, Mitchell, Dowd, Marsland and me. 'You will not present at this school with square cuts. Understood?'

'Yes, Brother.'

He leaves the room just as the bell rings.

The following night a few of us meet at the Theatre Royal. We're seeing *Doctor Zhivago*. I'm partnering Barbara, Flynn is with Vicki Westwood and O'Brien is with Sonia. It's a good crowd. We sit downstairs under the dress circle. It's a long film. Halfway through, my hand finds Barbara's hand. And we hold hands. I think Barbara is lovely. I walk her home. She lives right in town in Main Street, just up from the picture theatre. Above Wood and Wood Funeral Directors. I thank her for coming with me. She says she really enjoyed it.

'Would you like to do it again, sometime?'

'Yes. I would.'

We nod awkwardly and part ways. I walk home on air. Susan Morgan is no longer lingering in my mind. I almost want a carload of Slaters to appear so I can take them all on.

Flynn had set it up. 'You should ask Barbara.'

'Yeah?'

'Yeah.' So he asked her for me. He spoke to Deirdre, who spoke to Barbara and Barbara got back, through Deirdre. Flynn was as popular with the Public girls as he was with ours. And, as I said, he had introduced Sonia, a Public, to O'Brien.

•

O'Brien led a delegation of two, the other being Brewer, to argue the case for square cuts with the Bab. Square cuts were becoming an issue. It was a lunchtime meeting. There was to be no change in policy. Later that very lunchtime, the Bab had stern words with Doyle in the playground.

'Dad cuts my hair, Brother.'

This answer frustrated him.

I lied when he upbraided me. 'Mr Doyle cuts my hair, Brother. Mum can't afford a barber.' He turned very red in the face and walked off.

Doyle said, 'Look. He wants us to look like dicks. He wants us to have hair like him. I'm not having a short back and sides. Mum and Dad won't let me. They don't want me to look like a dick. He's going to have to talk to them and I bet he won't.'

And he didn't. Magically, the issue went away. Mr Doyle was apparently cutting most of the hair in the class.

•

Mum got a promotion at the typing pool at the Small Arms Factory. She was now in charge of twelve typists. She said that Mr White, her boss, liked 'her attitude'. She said Mr White is an amateur astronomer and that she told him she had been looking at Saturn recently. He was very impressed. Mum is on a roll. Mr Davies wants her to audition for *The Boy Friend*.

•

Doyle, Dean and I visit Sherb at the hospital. He actually looks a bit better. He tells us he's getting bored. 'A bloke has nothing to do. I walked around the hospital gardens yesterday, but I get very tired.'

We told him about the square-cut dispute. He didn't know what a square cut was. We told him. He thought about it. 'What does it bloody well matter what your hair looks like? It's unimportant. Boys, look carefully at the image of Saint John Baptist we have in the classroom. I think you could argue he wore what you could call a square cut.'

Dean said, 'That's brilliant, Brother.'

Doyle slipped him a few Benson & Hedges as we were leaving.

'Bless you, Doyle,' he whispered. 'A bloke can't smoke inside the hospital anymore. It's a new rule. The world is out of control, Doyle. Out of control. Thanks for thinking of me, boys. Keep the prayers up.'

•

O'Brien and Sonia were getting very close. They started meeting in town after school whenever footy training wasn't on. I was keen to catch up with Barbara, but she seemed to have a lot of work to do with her dad. Flynn would meet up with Vicki Westwood and together they played pinball at the milk bar beside the Theatre Royal listening to The Mamas and the Papas on the jukebox. Brewer and I would sometimes watch them. They had a brilliant technique whereby Flynn would work the right flipper and Vicki Westwood the left, with their free arms wrapped around each other and their heads touching. I can't speak for Brewer, but it made me feel jealous and I wanted more than anything to play pinball with Barbara just the same way.

•

The footy season was well underway. We hadn't lost a game, with wins being recorded against Portland, Wallerawang, Oberon and our real nemesis, Lithgow High School. When we played High School, Barbara and Deirdre came to watch. There was quite a good crowd. Too many Publics for my liking, but their heckling only firmed our resolve. I was happy with my game, managing three clear line breaks and setting up two tries for O'Brien. The Bab was most pleased that we hadn't allowed High School to score at all in the second half. 'Defence wins matches, men.' De La Salle, thirteen; High School, nine.

When we showered and changed I was fully expecting to meet up with Barbara and maybe go to the milk bar, but she'd gone. O'Brien and Sonia and Flynn and Vicki Westwood headed off together. I rode up and down Main Street looking for her and eventually gave up and headed home. Why hadn't she stayed? I spent a lot of the afternoon lying on my bed trying to get to the bottom of it.

At one stage Mum poked her head into my room and said, 'Are you all right?'

'Yeah,' I said, but she knew something wasn't right.

I went to the eight-thirty mass, hoping Barbara would be there. She was. She was with her dad and he caught me looking at her. And he caught her looking at me. After mass, people gathered around talking and I caught up with Dean and O'Brien while keeping a weather eye out for Barbara. Barbara's dad approached us. He wanted a word with me.

I followed him onto the footpath and he turned to me. 'No son of Bot Slaven is welcome within a thousand miles of any daughter of mine. Understood?'

I nodded.

'Are we clear?'

I nodded again. Then he walked off and gathered up Barbara, who was clearly embarrassed. I was shaken up.

Dean walked over to me. 'You all right?'

'Fuck'n Dad,' I said. 'Even when he's gone, he ruins everything.'

Dean didn't know what I was talking about. I didn't clarify. I was too upset for words. I was in tears walking to my bike.

As I rode home, I listed the things that gave me the shits about Dad. Number one is his costing me the second love of my life. Number two is Uncle Baz's jersey. Number three is his hitting Mum. Number four is his abandoning Mum. Number five is his being a no-hoper, which brands me a no-hoper, obviously. Hitting Mum should be number one, now I think about it.

When I got home, Mum was washing the sheets. It was a job of work. We had a copper that Mum hated and a mangle that she hated even more. Many a mum had got a hand caught in the mangle, often with disastrous results. Dean said his mum would get three mangled hands a week up at the hospital. Mrs Brewer had been mangled twice.

I helped Mum hang the sheets on the line and, out of the blue, it started raining and the wind changed direction, bringing all the dust from the huge coal heaps near the Genders mine, and the white sheets turned grey with black soot lines running down them. Mum was nearly in tears because they'd have to be washed again.

I didn't tell Mum what Barbara's dad had said. It was just a horrible day all round.

•

Maureen holds a newspaper up to us. It features a photograph of a winter landscape with what clearly holds the image of a man's face. 'This is a remarkable story, boys. What do you see? Brewer?'

'A face, Brother.'

'Yes. A face. But not just any face. The face of Jesus. This was taken by a Chinese photographer who was wandering through a snowfield in remote China. He heard a voice whisper in his ear, "Take a photo." So he did. And when he got home, so intrigued was he, that he developed the photograph immediately, and it was only then that he could see what it was he had photographed. He had photographed this, the face of Jesus. Miraculous.'

Doyle puts his hand up.

'Doyle?'

'How do we know it's Jesus, Brother? It could be Mike Nesmith.'

'Who is Mike Nesmith?'

'One of The Monkees, Brother.'

Maureen is furious. 'And who whispered in the ear of our Chinese photographer?'

Brewer says, 'A dead Monkees' fan?'

'That's enough! This is the face of Jesus. It can be the face of no other. To suggest it is, is nothing short of blasphemous. Do I make myself clear, Doyle?'

'Yes, Brother.'

'Brewer?'

'Yes, Brother.'

Dean puts his hand up.

'Yes, Dean?'

'This Jesus doesn't look like the Jesus on the shroud of Turin, Brother.'

Maureen looks at the image again. 'Well, Dean, that's a matter of opinion, and in my opinion, this is perfectly consistent with the Holy Shroud.'

We all knew it wasn't.

Brennan wants to know why Jesus didn't shave. 'Nobody shaved back then, Brennan. Where in God's name was somebody going to purchase a packet of Gillette Super Blue blades? Think about it.'

Doyle says, 'The Romans shaved, Brother. And the Greeks. Well before the time of Jesus. They must have been able to get blades from somewhere.'

Brewer says, 'They were all shaven in *Spartacus*. Kirk Douglas was.'

Brother Connor feels cornered.

Dean puts his hand up.

'Dean?'

'It's thought shaving has been around since the caveman, Brother. They used shells to scrape the hairs from the face. The Encyclopaedia Brita—'

'Yes. Well, that sounds like hearsay to me, Dean. At best. Who would know what cavemen got up to in their caves? Who could possibly know? Think about it.'

Dean shakes his head. Exasperated.

Brother Connor took a new position. 'Well, the Jews didn't shave.'

Hands are going up everywhere.

'Hands down. The discussion is closed.'

He folds up the newspaper with a disappointment that borders on anger. O'Brien has a holy card. It depicts Jesus as a clean-shaven, handsome white man. He holds it up. 'Artist's licence, O'Brien. Take out your exercise books.'

•

Shaving was in the ether. Dean had started shaving and I was starting to get what O'Brien's dad called 'bumfluff'. After school I rode up to the hospital and saw Sherb. He was in the garden, sitting in the sun with his eyes closed. One foot had come out of a loose-fitting slipper. I sat beside him. He opened his eyes and looked at me. 'Hello, Cec. It's so lovely to see you. You're a real sight for sore eyes.'

'Brother, when is the time right for a bloke to start shaving?'

He took his glasses out of his pyjama pocket and peered at me. 'I believe you're close, Cec. And you have come to just the right man.' He stood, slowly. 'Follow me.'

I did.

He shuffles into the hospital ward and finds his room. In a small cupboard beside his bed is a cardboard box. He opens it and takes out a small white porcelain bowl, a brush, a thin cake of white soap and a safety razor. I follow him into a large communal bathroom with five sinks and five small mirrors. He runs the water until it's hot and puts the plug in. He finds a facecloth in one of the shower booths.

'The secret to shaving is training your whiskers to grow the right way, especially those on your neck. Now, douse the cloth in the hot water to warm up your face. Hotter the better.'

While I did that, he wet the brush and lathered it with the soap in the porcelain bowl. He passed me the brush. 'Lather your face, Cec.' I did. 'Good man.' Then he passed me the razor. 'Now, puff your cheeks out and very carefully just draw the razor down. Make sure you don't cut yourself. Be gentle.'

I drew the blade down my puffed cheek.

'Good blow. Now rinse that off the razor and move on.' I did. 'That's the way. Keep your blows going in the one direction. Down. And that's the way the whiskers will grow.'

It only took a few minutes to have the job done. It was a bit tricky where the top lip joins the nose. 'Rinse the soap off and let's have a look at you.' I splashed fresh water all over my face and Sherb handed me his frayed white towel. I wiped my face and turned to him.

'That's the way. You could fill in for Tyrone Power. Once a fortnight will do you for a while.'

I looked at myself in the mirror. I looked fresh. 'Thanks, Brother.'

'You've made my day, Cec. Made my day. You haven't got a durry on you, I don't suppose?'

'Sorry, Brother.'

As I was leaving, he gave me fifty cents and asked me to buy him a packet of Rothmans king size. There was a corner shop not far from the hospital. I had the cigarettes in his hand, with change, in minutes. 'God bless you, boy,' he said, and headed back out to the garden for a puff.

Mum looked at me closely. 'What is it about you, Roy?'

I told her. She was teary. She cuddled me, kissed me on the forehead. 'I find it hard to believe my little boy has just had a shave. Makes me feel old.'

'You're not old, Mum. Look at Mrs Dean or Mrs Brewer. You're still a girl.' And with that she smiled and put the radio on.

She had four orders for dresses. Mrs Leslie's 'tent', as she called it, was finished.

Chapter Fourteen

'Boys, the secret to marriage is that each must put in one hundred and fifty percent, so that if one hundred percent is lost, there is still two hundred percent to fall back on.'

BROTHER HUGH CORCORAN

'And as for sex. Boys, it's just like sneezing.'

BROTHER CONNOR

It's Saturday morning. It's half past five and I'm riding over to Doyle's to watch a special broadcast on television. Doyle said it's called *Our World* and The Beatles will be playing live. It's the second satellite broadcast in history. Doyle watched a bit of the first one from Montreal, which was ordinary, but said I'd be mad if I didn't watch this one.

I arrive in his backyard and he quickly ushers me in to the lounge room. The television is on. The Beatles are on very soon. Mr Doyle is standing in front of the set with a bowl of rolled oats and a spoon. Cath is in her pyjamas, sitting on the chair Grandma usually sits on. She's eating cheese on toast.

Doyle hands me a bowl, pours some cornflakes into it, before pouring some for himself. We add our own milk and stand beside Mr Doyle. Doyle's mum must still be in bed. No sign of Jen. No sign of Tony Doyle. The house was quiet but for the television.

Then The Beatles come on. 'All You Need is Love.' It is fantastic. Immediately memorable. The Beatles seem supremely confident. John and Paul chew gum while they sing.

'What is it with the timing, Dad?'

'A three-four bar in a four-four time signature.'

Mr Doyle counts it out to Doyle. He gets it.

'Wow. That's really nice.'

Doyle notices the faces in the crowd sitting at The Beatles' feet. 'The Stones are there to pay homage.'

The Beatles finish. The television is turned off. We feel we have been connected to the world. Mr Doyle is amazed we were watching something live from England. He puts some toast on and boils the jug. He sings 'All You Need is Love'. He stops what he's doing and looks at Doyle.

'At the ending. A bit of Glen Miller.'

Doyle says he heard 'Greensleeves'.

'And "She Loves You".'

Doyle nods.

'Incredible,' says Mr Doyle. 'Just incredible. A signal bouncing off a satellite in space.'

'At the speed of light,' says Doyle.

Our world in a lounge room in Lithgow is linked to London with immediacy and impact.

I ride home thinking I should get some Kellogg's Corn Flakes for me and Mum. Had never had cornflakes before. Really nice.

•

Flynn has made an astonishing discovery. It's lunchtime and me, Flynn and O'Brien are throwing torpedo passes to each other on the edge of the oval. Vicki Westwood had taken Flynn to the public library to show him a book on the mechanics of sex.

'Did you know that when you ejaculate, forty million spermatozoa are released into the world?'

The passing stops. O'Brien says, 'Bullshit.'

'How many?' I ask.

'Forty million. At least. True. Bet you it's true.' He puts his hand out. 'Come on. Bet you. Fifty cents.'

Neither O'Brien nor me take the bet. He might be right. We need to find out. It seems implausible. We need to track down Dean or Doyle.

They are together in the First Form classroom, looking at the map of the world on the wall and discussing countries in Eastern Europe while eating sandwiches. Neither of them knows if it's true or not. We leave the classroom as a group. Dean spots Harold who is doing playground duty. Harold is looking

John Doyle

at a Volkswagen manual that came with his recently purchased second-hand Volkswagen, which we all reckon is a joke.

Dean puts the Flynn proposition to him. He looks up, adjusts his glasses and says, 'Yeah, that'd be right. Might be a bit more than that actually. Closer to a hundred million. With bulls it's more. A good breeder will ejaculate hundreds of millions of spermatozoa. Probably the same with pigs, but I don't know. Why?'

'Just wondering, Sir. Thank you.'

Doyle sees implications. 'To masturbate is to be a mass murderer. Look at Benson. How many people has he killed? Many, many more than Hitler. Benson is capable of killing four hundred million people a day.'

Dean agrees. He wants to ask Maureen about it. That afternoon, he does. His hand is up as Brother Connor sweeps into the classroom.

'Dean?'

'An ethical question, Brother.'

'Ethical? I'm all ears, Dean.'

'Brother, is it true that to wantonly ejaculate is to squander life?'

'This is a highly prepared question, Dean. Should I be looking for a trap here? If it is masturbation you are talking about then, yes, it is a squandering of life, as you put it.'

Dean presses. 'Is squandering life murder, Brother?'

'What does your conscience tell you, Dean?'

'I want to know what the law is here, Brother.'

'Which law? There is divine law, canon law, magisterial law and civil law. I think masturbation is an act of murder, but the civil courts don't think so. Does that answer your question?'

Dean sits down. Doyle puts his hand up.

'Doyle?'

'Are you aware how many spermatozoa are produced in a single ejaculation, Brother?'

'Not a clue, Doyle, and I couldn't care less, be it one or three hundred.'

'Forty million, Brother.'

'Don't be ridiculous, Doyle.'

Flynn stands and proffers his hand. 'Bet you he's right, Brother. A dollar.'

Brother Connor retreats. 'Sit down, thank you, Flynn.'

Maureen took his waddy out of his pocket. 'On your feet, Benson.'

Benson stands. 'Name three types of triangle.'

Benson looks at his hand. 'Equilateral, right-angled and isosceles.'

Doyle and Benson exchange a nod. The Tropics applaud. Followed by the Tundra and some of the Temperate.

'That's enough! Exercise books out now!' He picks up some chalk and begins writing equations on the board at a furious pace.

•

Mum is pacing in front of the fire in the lounge room. She is very nervous. She asks me to 'lie low'. Father Keogh is coming around at seven o'clock. She doesn't say why. When there is a knock at the door, I disappear. She lets Father Keogh in. He's not alone. He's joined by Father Kane, Father Grannal and Father Connaughton, from the Portland parish. They sit around the kitchen table. From the hall, I can hear what's going on.

'Mrs Slaven, I have brought Father Kane and Father Connaughton because of their expertise in the matter you wish to raise. Father Grannal, you know, as a most practical priest. Now. Annulment is a very serious business and there must be clear grounds in one of three key areas. Father?'

Then Father Kane begins. 'The grounds are lack of capacity, lack of consent or lack of form. Now. Lack of capacity. Were you over the age of fourteen?'

Mum says, 'Yes. I was seventeen.'

'Does your husband have the ability to procreate?'

'You know he does.'

'Was your husband a cleric at the time of the marriage?'

'Clearly not.'

'Is he a close relative?'

'No.'

Father Connaughton says, 'There is therefore no lack of capacity.'

Father Kane continues. 'Now. Lack of consent. At the time, did you understand what marriage was, Mrs Slaven?'

'Yes, I did.'

'Did your husband enter the marriage without the intention of fidelity?'

'What does that mean, Father?'

'Did he get up to any tomcatting, Mrs Slaven?'

'You'd have to ask him, but not to my knowledge.'

'Hmm. No grounds for a lack of consent appeal, then. And so to lack of form. Were you a non-Catholic at the time of the marriage?'

'Yes.'

There's a bit of whispering among the priests I can't hear. Then Father Grannal says, 'Why did you marry the man, Mrs Slaven?'

'I was eight months pregnant, Father.'

Father Kane injects himself into the conversation. 'I want you to think about this question very seriously, Mrs Slaven. Have you been baptised a Christian?'

'I'm not sure, Father.'

'You see, if you were not baptised, a dispensation would have to have been given by the bishop for the marriage to proceed. Was dispensation ever sought? Or were you baptised into the church prior to the wedding?'

'No, I wasn't and I can't recall any dispensation being sought or given.'

There is silence for a minute or so.

'Well,' says Father Kane, 'there may well be grounds for lack of form. This will need to be referred to an ecclesiastical tribunal.'

'There will be costs, Mrs Slaven,' says Father Keogh, 'between three and four hundred dollars. And the procedure will take eighteen months or so. So. So, it is a matter that must not be entered into lightly. In the meantime, I will write to the priest who conducted the marriage and see what the records show as a means of getting the ball rolling.'

'And how much will that cost, Father?'

'Should you choose to return to the sacraments, it will cost you nothing.'

'And if I don't return to the sacraments?'

'It will cost you your immortal soul.'

Father Grannal says, 'Tell him to come home, Mrs Slaven. Make him feel welcome. Give your boy the father he needs. You're still a young woman, there may well be time to bring three or four more souls into the world.'

All the priests agree with this.

'Well said, Father.'

'Wise words, Father.'

Eventually they leave.

'Did you hear any of that?'

I nod.

'It's not often I say this, but I need a drink.' Mum takes a bottle of whisky Dad was given by Uncle Baz for Christmas out of the cupboard. She unscrews the cap and pours herself a small glassful.

She sits by the fire and sips. 'It's so important that you understand that, while I regret much of what has happened with your father, I have no regrets about you. You make me as proud as any mother could possibly be. If I didn't have you,

I would have nothing. But I have to ask you, how you would feel if I was to divorce?'

I worked the fire with the poker. 'I want you to be happy, Mum. If divorce makes you happy, I'm all for it. It's been so much better with Dad away. I'd like him to stay away. For good.'

Mum stood up, grabbed another glass, poured a thimbleful and handed it to me. 'A toast to the future, Roy. Our future.'

We clink our glasses. I sip and almost lose my breath, it's so strong.

'Are you okay, my darling?'

I recover. Mum kisses me on the forehead. I tell her it's much stronger than the altar wine Brewer was selling.

'What?'

I tell her the story. She laughs. 'That is just so naughty. That's got to be sinful. Surely.'

Chapter Fifteen

'Of course you must be fit. But a tennis match
is won or lost almost entirely in the mind.'

Herbert Wilson, Tennis Coach

'It is impossible to please God if you do not
live on friendly terms with others.'

Saint John Baptist

Brother Michael was keen to get some tennis going again. There were no competitions happening so all courts were available. We agreed on a Sunday game if the weather permitted.

Sunday arrives and the weather is good. At two o'clock we set up the net on Lithgow's number one show court. It's near Brewer's place. Brother Michael is in good spirits, obviously happy to get out of the house, and we're excited to be on the court where the greats have played. It was Brother Michael's idea. I partner Brother Michael and Dean plays with Doyle.

Brother Michael makes the observation that no matter where
you are in Lithgow you are aware of the hills. 'It's good for the
spirits, isn't it, being reminded of nature?' We agree.

The game splutters along. Dean still has little control, Doyle
has a reliable forehand and Brother Michael, while fit and
willing, has few skills. I do what I normally do and try to hit
the ball that plays to Dean and Doyle's strengths. Doyle makes
a point of hitting the ball only to Brother Michael, and usually
to his backhand, which is woeful, and Brother Michael keeps
apologising to me when he frames the ball over the back line,
or into the net.

'Sorry, Roy.'

'You're right, Brother,' I say.

I notice the black Zephyr pulls up by the court. Brian Lawson
gets out and approaches us. 'Hey! Have you got permission to
play on this court?'

We stop. Brother Michael takes the lead. 'Why? Is there a
problem?'

'You've got to get permission.'

Doyle says, 'We've got permission.'

'Who from?'

'The mayor.'

Brother Michael is embarrassed. Brian ignores Doyle and
looks at me. 'I'm the secretary of this tennis club. And I'm the
club champion and I say who can use this court and who can't.'

Brother Michael is very apologetic. 'I'm sorry. We were

of the understanding that if the court wasn't being used, we could use it.'

'And you are?'

'I teach these boys. At La Salle. We'll certainly leave now if there's a problem.'

Brian smiles. 'I'll tell you what. This boy here owes me money. Fourteen dollars. I'm going to go home and change and be back here in ten minutes. If you, Tiger, can take a game off me, the debt is waived and you can play here. Have we got a deal? Or are you a lying chicken?'

I shrug. 'Deal.'

Brian lights up. 'You've made my day. I'm going to give you a lesson in humility, young man.' And he heads off.

Brother Michael looks at me. He is confused. 'What's this about?'

'He's been trying to crack onto Mum. She has no interest, obviously, she's married, but it hasn't stopped him.'

'And the fourteen dollars?'

'He's making that up.'

Doyle looks sheepish. Brother Michael is utterly baffled by it all. He senses from Doyle's reaction that something is going on. We keep our game going and, fifteen minutes later, Brian returns.

He walks onto the court with white sandshoes, white shorts and a neat polo top bearing a Lacoste logo. He carries a bag holding four racquets and a canister of new balls. He takes out two racquets and hits them against each other testing the tension of the strings. He makes his selection and opens the canister of balls. He stretches his arms, jumps up and down on the spot and says, 'I don't need a hit up. Which end do you want, Tiger?'

I choose an end and he says, 'Suits me. I'll serve.'

He wins his service game easily. I have a bit of trouble reading his serve, which swings and cuts off the court. We change ends and I serve. Each of my serves lands in his hitting zone and he puts away two clean winners. There follows two short rallies and I haven't won a point. 'Two–love,' he broadcasts.

I decide to stand a bit further back when receiving to give myself a bit more time, and very quickly I start being able to read his body language and can predict the direction of the ball as he strikes it. I return each ball with interest and he is struggling. He's down love–forty and is looking very serious. He double faults trying to put too much speed on the ball. I win the game.

'Happy to keep going?' I ask. I only had to win one game.

Doyle shouts out, 'One. Two. Slaven to serve.'

Brian is furious with himself. He bumps me with his shoulder at the change of ends. Obviously he's keen to continue.

I serve at his body. He hates it and dollies the ball back for an easy put away. I serve at his body again with the identical result. Doyle starts announcing the score and commentating on the match. 'Thirty–love. Slaven beginning to impose himself here.'

'Shut up!' yells Brian. His next return gives me the first opportunity to reveal my top-spin forehand. He is seriously amazed by it. He shakes his head and I draw level at two games all.

'I think young Slaven has got this bloke's measure,' says Doyle.

Brian glares at him and hits a ball out of the court over the railway line in frustration.

'And we're now one ball down,' Doyle comments.

Brian approaches Doyle. 'One more smartarse comment and you are banned from the courts. For all time. Understand?'

Brother Michael urges Doyle to be quiet. He is.

Very quickly I'm serving for the set. I've found a groove. If the top-spin forehand unsettled him, the top-spin backhand really has him doubting his sanity. The other thing I notice is, the harder he tries, the better I play. The harder he hits the ball, the faster it gets back to him.

I serve a clear ace. He calls it a fault. Brother Michael says, 'No. That was well in.' I say I don't care and ace him again with my second ball. A top-spin forehand drive, a drop shot and a backhand top-spin drive into the corner and I've won the set six games to two.

Brian packs his racquets away. He is nearly in tears of rage.

'Looks like we're allowed to play here,' I say.

Brian says nothing. He walks back to the Zephyr and drives off.

'Well. We've got three new balls,' says Doyle.

Brother Michael is completely astonished. 'I didn't know you could play like that, Roy.'

'Nor did I.'

And really, I didn't know. And I'm thinking I can't wait to tell Mum.

'He'll be mortified,' was Mum's response. 'I'd have loved to have seen the game. Six–two?'

I nodded.

'How did he win two?' And she laughed. She cuddled me. She kissed me on the forehead. I slept well.

•

It's a quiet night. Mum's working on her dresses on the kitchen table. I'm trying to read *Great Expectations*. It's just not interesting. Jack Connolly is setting a test on it. The radio is on. 2LT, 'Requests' with Terry Preece. After an ad for 'Finley's for Fine Furniture', Terry starts talking to someone on the telephone. 'Now, this is a great story, if it's true. But someone who swears it is, is a caller named Eric. Eric, what's the story?

'I was walking by the district tennis court yesterday, Terry, and I saw the best match I've seen in years.'

I say to Mum, 'That's Doyle.'

Mum gives it her attention. 'The young Slaven kid, he gave our district champion an absolute towelling. Six–two. And this kid's only been playing for five minutes, Terry. He's a champion of the future.'

'Slaven, you say?'

'Roy Slaven.'

'Well, Roy Slaven, this song's been requested for you. Thanks, Eric.' The Beatles' 'Baby, You're A Rich Man' is played.

Mum says, 'Is he allowed to do that? Make up a name?'

'I don't think there's a law against it, Mum. Yet.'

Mum's really excited. 'You're famous, Roy. The boy who beat the man.'

Mum was right. Someone from *The Lithgow Mercury* is at the school and I'm called out of class by Brother Hugh to talk to Len.

Len is very energetic. Friendly. He swings a large camera from his shoulder and puts it on the ground, frees his arms to take notes with a pencil on a small writing pad. His first question is, 'Is it true that you beat Brian Lawson?'

'Yeah.'

'Was he trying?'

'I think so.'

'Would you play him again?'

'Yes.'

He takes my photograph.

So now there is an article in the paper. 'Boy issues challenge', which wasn't really true. It was Len's idea. Mum likes the photograph of me that supports the article. Then Brother Michael is interviewed by Len. He says, in his view, Brian was definitely trying and Roy won, hands down. There's another article. No photograph. 'Man of God is convinced'.

Brian Lawson is interviewed by *The Mercury*. They use the photograph of him holding up the A-grade trophy he had won. Beside it is the photograph of me in my school uniform. According to the article, he said that he felt a lot of sympathy for a boy whose father had walked out on the family, and had let me win. When he was asked about a rematch he is quoted as saying, 'He can enter any of our tournaments and, should he qualify, I am quite happy to play him.'

Mum is furious when she reads this. 'How dare he?'

Len seems to be a dog with a bone. He's back at the school and I'm talking to him again. He says he'd been talking to the manager at Finley's and they were prepared to sponsor a match between me and Brian Lawson. He takes a photo of me holding Doyle's Pancho Gonzales tennis racquet. It's a page three story.

Mr White, the boss of the typing pool, gets interested. After talking to Mum, he talks to his boss and there is another article in the paper saying the Lithgow Small Arms Factory is supporting the Finley's challenge and will donate fifty dollars to the district tennis club should the event be staged. There is a photograph of a soldier standing with a locally produced FN rifle to support the article.

Brian has become the subject of some ridicule. He's being accosted in the street. 'Scared of the Slaven kid, are you, champ?' There's another article in the paper. Finley's is offering a brand new Slazenger racquet to the winner. There is a photograph of Ray Doyle standing outside Finley's in Main Street holding the new Slazenger racquet. By the end of that week, the prize had been upgraded to a new Simpson washing machine. A photograph of Ray Doyle with the washing machine supports the article. The Finley's ad in *The Mercury* mentioned they were proud sponsors of the Finley's Tennis Challenge. Father Keogh uses the challenge in a long-winded David and Goliath metaphor in his sermon at the eight-thirty mass.

When Doyle and I visit Sherb, even he is aware of it. 'Is he a Catholic? This Lawson fellow?'

'I don't think so, Brother.'

'Good. I didn't like the sound of him.'

I ride home by the Commercial Hotel where patrons holding glasses of beer spill out onto the street. One shouts, 'There's Bot's boy!'

'Arsehole,' I think.

Bracey's, the department store, is not to be outdone by Finley's, and offers a new HMV television set as part of the prize. A photograph of me standing outside Bracey's in Main Street supports the article.

On Monday's front page, down the bottom is the headline 'At last! Lawson agrees!' The match had to be played on a Sunday because of my Rugby League commitments. On the Saturday night before the match there's a knock on our door. Mum answers. It's Ray Doyle from Finley's. He has the new racquet for me to use. Mum says, 'What a lovely man.'

Normally, when I have a big match coming up, I get worked up and have trouble sleeping, but on this occasion I enjoyed the sleep of the dead, mainly because it had been a surprisingly hard footy match against Portland who had a new forward from Kandos called 'Tank'. Tank was really hard to stop. We scratched our way to a thirteen to ten win. O'Brien scored in the dying minutes of the game. My pass found the gap and he found the ball. But we worked hard for the win. Especially in defence.

Mum and I walk to the courts. It's a cool but sunny day and there is almost no wind at all. When we arrive, the viewing stand is almost full. The car park is full and Len from *The Mercury* is there to greet us. I look at the crowd. I see O'Brien and Sonia, Flynn and Vicki Westwood, Dean, Mr and Mrs Dean, Doyle, Brewer, Mr and Mrs Brewer, Mr and Mrs Goggin, Brother Connor, Brother Hugh, Brother Michael, Harold, Father Keogh, Father Kane, Father Grannal, Sister Geraldine, Ray Doyle and many, many others. Quite a few Publics. There would have been three hundred people all up. Maybe more. Mum said most of 'her girls' from the typing pool were there. Mr White was there. Mrs Leslie was there, wearing the dress Mum had made for her. It was standing room only.

There was a lot of applause when I stepped onto the court. Len gets Brian Lawson and me to stand together by the net with our racquets and he takes what he calls 'the official photograph'. Herbie Wilson, the district tennis club president, tosses a coin and I call correctly and invite Brian to serve.

Brian looks nervous. He bounces the ball in readiness to serve and it hits the toe of his sandshoe and rolls towards the net. A ball boy retrieves it and throws it back to him.

'Good start, Brian!' someone shouts. Probably Doyle. The crowd erupts into laughter.

Brian starts with a double fault. He nurses the next serve in and we have quite an entertaining rally. Well, it was entertaining for me, because I didn't have to move much at all as I was running him from side to side until he started to flag. A neat drop shot finished the point. There is applause.

Brian changes his racquet.

Brewer shouts, 'I hope that's the lucky racquet, Brian!' Laughter.

Brian pauses and glares at the crowd. His face betrays his hatred for them all. He sends down a ferocious serve. All I can do is throw my racquet at it, which catches the ball and sends it back at an angle the crowd cannot believe. Nor can Brian. Nor can I, to be honest. I am loving this new racquet. Love–forty. A firm winner that catches the line after a shaky serve gives me the first game.

We change ends. I try a new technique. When tossing the ball to serve, I throw it higher and angle it further into the court which means I need to push off my knees and am in the air when I strike it. In the paper, Len described it as the fastest serve Lithgow had ever seen. It was well past Brian before he was aware of it. There is applause from the crowd. The next serve is just as fast and it cannons into the cabana directly behind Brian and ricochets flush into the back of his head. There is a gasp from the crowd. Then gales of laughter. The ricochet was to become a feature of the afternoon.

Brian is now arguing with Herbie Wilson. He's saying my service action is illegal. Herb is a coach. He knows the rules. He deems my serve to be fine. The second ricochet hits Brian in the bum. He jumps in surprise.

John Doyle

O'Brien shouts, 'I'd be looking at his racquet, Brian. I don't think dynamite is legal.' More laughter. Two more aces and I'm two games up.

'When are you going to win a point, Brian?' Doyle again. Much crowd laughter. Brother Connor has a word to him. I spot Barbara in the crowd. I think she catches my eye. She is sitting with Deirdre and a girl I see at netball whose name I don't know. My heart soars.

I set myself the challenge. Brian Lawson is not going to win one point. He nearly did. In the sixth game he had me out of position. I don't know how it happened, I have forgotten. The court was wide open. All he needed to do was get the ball over the net. Instead he netted it.

Brian Lawson is in shock. And disbelief. His rage with himself is almost on a par with Doyle's sister. His senses of reason and proportion have sailed well away. He screams at his racquet and hits his forehead with it. He lashes out at a ball with his foot and it sails into the crowd, hitting Mrs Leslie. She's shaken up but okay. Brian Lawson is unaware of this as he continues to remonstrate with himself.

I wait for him to settle. It's set point. My first serve is good and we parry stroke for stroke. I unleash the top-spin backhand, follow it in and put away the simplest of volleys.

There is bedlam. A roar from the crowd and car horns blaring. A passing train blows its whistle.

Six–love. He didn't win a point. It was to be the best of three sets, but he concedes. 'Too good,' he mutters.

210

Dean and Doyle lift me into the air and the crowd is on its feet. Herbie Wilson settles them down and thanks everyone for coming and reminds them that the club is always looking for new members. He adds, 'What we have seen here today is the birth of a champion. We will follow his career with great interest.'

When the applause dies down again, Ray Doyle is introduced and he congratulates me and lets people know that the racquet I was using was a gift from Finley's, and the Simpson washing machine would be delivered and installed by week's end. Applause. I see Mum and she is in tears. Then the bloke from Bracey's goes on a bit long but ends up saying the HMV eighteen-inch television set would be delivered on Thursday. A man in a suit from the Small Arms Factory hands Herbie Wilson a cheque for fifty dollars.

As the crowd disperses, Len takes photographs of me with the bloke from the factory, me with the bloke from Bracey's and me with Ray Doyle. Then me with Herbie Wilson, who gets me aside and urgently peppers me with questions, none of which I can satisfactorily answer. 'Who showed you that grip? How do you control the top-spin? Who taught you that? Where have you been?'

All I can say is, 'Usually the ball goes where I want it to. I just see it.' And I shrug. And then Mum is beside me and a lot of people I don't know and some want my autograph. It takes ages to make our way home.

Mum is bursting with excitement as we walk home. I'm ruing the missed opportunity of seeing Barbara. She'd left by the time the well-wishing had finished. I wondered if her dad knew she was there.

Mum's talking about some of the points and what some people were saying but I wasn't hearing a word. I was imagining what Barbara might have thought of the match and if ever I would be allowed to talk to her again.

A few people honk and wave from the open windows of a Fiat that passes us. Mum is over the moon at the prospect of a washing machine. I'm over the moon at the prospect of a television set. The story is featured on the 2LT news that night and we listen while we devour our toasted cheese and tomato sandwiches.

'I might get some mustard,' I say. 'Doyle uses mustard on his toasted sandwiches.'

Mum says, 'Don't you need ham? With mustard?'

'You're right, Mum. We need ham as well.'

It was strangely unsettling hearing myself talked about on the news. Mum turned the radio up as far as it would go. She wasn't unsettled at all. She was beaming.

•

'Pointless Champ Humiliated' is the back-page headline of the Monday *Mercury*. There's the 'official photograph', and a photograph of Mum she didn't know was being taken. She looks like a movie star. She wears the perfect smile. The accident of light gives her a halo. It's a face that melts the heart of Lithgow. In the street, some are calling her 'Roy's mum'. She tells me she loves being Roy's mum. She said I was being talked about in the typing pool. 'Your ears should be burning.' She kisses me on the forehead.

Chapter Sixteen

'Mea culpa, mea culpa, mea maxima culpa.'

TRIDENTINE MASS

'I'm a cowboy, I'm a cowboy, I'm a Mexican cowboy.'

ONE OF THE CULLEN GIRLS

'It's Brother, not bra. We don't wear them. Understood?'

BROTHER HUGH CORCORAN

'Roy's mum' has what she is calling a 'call back' with Des Davies for a role in *The Boy Friend*. But there's singing involved. She is instructed by Kathy Wilson to drop into Tony Doyle's house and he will assess her singing ability.

At school, Brother Connor's attitude towards me is odd. 'Well, boys. Well. We now have a champion in our midst. What a pity it is that our champion doesn't apply himself to his schoolwork with the same diligence he so obviously does to hitting a small white ball over a net. I suppose you'll expect now to be sitting in the Tropics? Well, Slaven, as far as I'm concerned, you will stay a Tundra man until you start taking your education seriously. Understood?'

'Yes, Brother.'

'Who knows? There might be a brain in that head of yours, Slaven. I'd love to see some evidence.'

At lunchtime, Flynn, O'Brien and I look at how the new classrooms are coming along. The bricklayers are close to completing the walls of what will become the new Third Form and Fourth Form classrooms. I confide in them what Barbara's father had said to me and seek advice.

'I wouldn't get her into trouble,' says O'Brien. Flynn suggests that O'Brien should talk to his father and get him to talk to Barbara's father after mass and to point out what a good bloke I was. 'Lie, you mean?' says O'Brien, with a wink.

'All is fair in love and war, mate. That's what Errol reckons.'

Harold's on playground duty and he orders us away from the building site. 'Hey. Flynn and co. You know the rules.'

'Sorry, Sir,' says Flynn, and we join the Tropics and Tundra crowd down by the toilets where Doyle is doing his Brian Lawson impersonation.

'What he's doing isn't legal, Herbie. He's got to keep one foot on the ground. It's illegal, Herbie. Help me, Herbie. He's making me look stupid, Herbie. Herbie? Am I stupid, Herbie? I'm looking like a dick here, Herbie.'

It goes down well. Benson says he didn't know the match was on. As the bell rings, O'Brien quietly says to me, 'Do you want me to talk to Dad?'

'Thanks, mate. No. I'll work it out.'

After school, I tell Doyle that Mum will be visiting his place. He says I should come as well, so at about half past four we arrive at Doyle's. Tony Doyle answers the front door and he's very friendly, he knows Mum from the RSL Club. He calls her Paulette. He nods to me, and we're briefly introduced. We go into the lounge room where the lounge chairs have been moved to allow access to the upright piano. Tony Doyle is a bit like a showman. 'There's a lot going on in this house, Paulette, you won't be bored.'

Jen is rocking on the lounge. I say hello to her. 'Hello,' she says, without looking at me or breaking stride with her rocking.

'Hello,' says Mum. She is ignored.

Tony Doyle says, 'Say hello to Paulette, Jen.'

Without looking at Mum, she says, 'Hello, Paulette.' That's as far as the conversation is going.

'Lovely home,' says Mum. SHe looks at the landscape paint-ings on the wall. 'Who's the artist?'

'Dad,' says Tony Doyle. The shop bell rings. Mum's startled. Tony Doyle tells Mum to ignore it and he sits at the piano. The sheet music is open at a song called 'Poor Little Pierrette'. Mum takes off her overcoat. I can tell she's very nervous.

'I need to hear your range,' he says. He plays middle C and she quietly sings it. 'Good,' he says. He goes up an octave and Mum sings it. 'Very good.' He then plays the chords and sings with the melody. It sounds a bit drippy to me.

He then stops and says, 'I'm going to sing the harmony, which is what you'll be singing.' He then sings the harmony line. Then they sing the harmony line together. He asks Mum to sing it alone, which she does. 'That's good, Paulette. Now. I'll sing the melody and you stay with the harmony. Two, three, and . . .' They sing it together. It's beautiful. He stops. 'Yeah. You've got an ear and that's all that matters. An ear, you are born with. It can't be taught.'

While this is going on, Mrs Doyle flashes up out of the shop in through the kitchen and flies back down again. A few times. The shop bell rings every few seconds. Doyle wanders in from somewhere.

Together we leave them to it and go out into the backyard. A fresh load of coal has been dumped half in, half out, of the concrete bunker and in the back lane. He's been shovelling the rest of it in. He keeps going while we chat. I wanted to talk to him about Barbara's dad but decide against it in case he exacts some revenge on Barbara's dad with dog turds, or something even worse. We talk about what I might watch on the television when it arrives, apart from *Peyton Place*. He says *Star Trek* is pretty good. It's his dad's favourite show. It's on Channel Nine. At this stage it's anyone's guess what channels we'll be able to get.

Shortly after, Tony Doyle's at the back door. 'Your mum's done, mate.'

I head inside, leaving Doyle with the last of the coal to shovel, and I can tell Mum is pretty excited. Youngest sister Cath has been watching it all and is happy the session is over. She pushes the lounge chairs back into position. She's setting up for television. Jen is hovering by the refrigerator, rocking from side to side and flapping her arms, waiting for someone to undo the belt. The bell is still ringing every few seconds. Grandma appears through a door, ready for television. Mum puts her overcoat on and we're ushered out through the front door by Tony Doyle.

On the walk home, Mum says confidentially, 'He thinks I could be cast as Fay.'

'Does Fay do much, Mum?'

'I don't think so. I hope not. Is Mrs Doyle always that busy?'

'I think so.'

Mum shakes her head. 'And what is to become of that poor unfortunate girl?'

I shrug.

Then, 'That's a very busy house.'

•

A bloke from Bracey's drops off the television set. Mum squeals. It's in a big cardboard box. Together we take it out and place it on a timber fruit box in the corner of the lounge room. There is a booklet with instructions and we quickly discover two problems. We don't have a power point in the lounge room and we don't have an antenna. We set it up on the kitchen bench where there is a power point and Mum turns it on. I pray for a miracle. It's just snow on every channel. Mum says she can pick up an extension cord, long enough to get it into the lounge room. But the antenna is a bit more difficult. The average height of antennae in Lithgow is about forty feet and requires serious professionals to install it. We're disappointed. Me more than Mum.

Ray Doyle arrives the following afternoon with a bloke called John and together they skilfully muscle the copper and mangle out into the street before positioning the new Simpson washing machine in the laundry, which fortunately has a power point. Ray Doyle makes sure the machine is balanced and stable by making adjustments to the feet and then gets Mum to load up the machine with clothes. Then he turns it on. Mum is most impressed. He asks me who has been giving me tennis lessons and can't believe I've never had one from a professional coach. 'Just Mum in the backyard.'

'You're the most natural tennis player I've ever seen. If you stick with it you will be playing Davis Cup well before you're twenty.'

Mum says how proud she is of me and thanks Ray Doyle for being so generous.

'You're at the typing pool now, aren't you, Mrs Slaven?'

'I am.'

'It's a very good job. And you're renting the house from Peter Croker?'

Mum nods.

'I know Peter pretty well. Let me talk to him. It might be in his interest to put an antenna on the house, and to put a few more power points in. Leave it with me.'

Ray Doyle and John leave, taking away the copper and mangle in the back of the Finley's Holden utility. The same utility that picked us up in the rain on Sherb's walk. Mum really likes Ray Doyle. 'What a gentle, lovely man.'

Mum and me stand in the cold in the laundry and closely watch the washing machine go though its cycles. It's not quick. When it's finished, Mum is astounded. 'Feel these clothes, Roy, they're nearly dry.' She sniffs the washing. 'And smell it!' I do. It smells like lemon. We look at each other. We have a taste for the first time of what it's like to live the good life. Mum kisses me on the forehead. She needs a handkerchief to wipe her eyes.

We go in and I light the fire and Mum looks in the cupboard for something in a can we can heat up and put on toast. She sings. I wait until she stops before putting on the radio. She finds a can of asparagus spears that came in a box of cans, mainly without labels, given to us when Dad was here. Neither of us has ever eaten asparagus spears. She shows me the can. I shrug.

We ate it because we were hungry. We both agreed. Asparagus spears? Never again.

Chapter Seventeen

'Brother, could God build a rock that's
too heavy for Him to lift?'

<small>BREWER</small>

'Arm. Arm is cranky. Cranky arm.'

<small>JEN</small>

Doyle has had *Sergeant Pepper's Lonely Hearts Club Band* for weeks but we haven't had a chance to listen to it together. Doyle thinks it's brilliant. The bass playing is the standout feature, in his opinion. Flynn has heard the whole album. He likes it. O'Brien hasn't heard it. Dean hasn't. Benson hasn't even heard of the album. Brewer says he's heard it but no one believes him. Brother Michael would like to hear it. Jack Connolly says he hasn't heard it but has a small collection of Perry Como records he might bring in one day to brighten us up. Brother Connor says he has absolutely no interest in The Beatles' music.

John Doyle

'Music is at its finest when it's in the hands of those who know what they are doing. Those who are musically trained. Give a monkey a typewriter and sooner or later it will write a sentence. But does the sentence have meaning? Is the monkey, no matter how clever, going to write something that is of any interest to me or anyone else in this room? Do I want to hear some recorded noise from untrained monkeys? We are much, much closer to hearing the voice of God in a Brahms lullaby than we are with "I Wanna Hold Your Hand". Sergeant somebody and his lonely band of peppered hearts is just the sort of mindless gibberish I would expect from our monkey with the typewriter. You couldn't pay me to listen to it.'

It's Saturday night and I arrive at Doyle's just after half past eight. He shows me the *Sergeant Pepper* cover and I look at it while he packs up his books. He's finished his homework. Part of me envies crawlers. They're organised in a way that is beyond me. He asks me about *Great Expectations* and I can't add much to the discussion because I'm finding it too boring to finish. He says it's about class and deceit. He talks about the English class system and how Australia is more about egalitarianism.

His grandma is off to bed and stops to listen to us. For some reason she seems annoyed at whatever Doyle is saying. 'Egalitarianism sounds too much like Communism for my liking. Ask yourself whether you would like to live under the jackboot of Brezhnev. Have you learnt your kings and queens of England yet?'

'No, Ma.'

'Well, you're being taught nothing. Charles Dickens is a very fine storyteller, but it's just a story, no more, no less. Have you done the milk crates?'

'Yes, Ma.'

She looks at me. 'Try and talk some sense into him. He goes on with so much nonsense.'

'I'll do my best,' I say.

'What's that you're looking at?'

'*Sergeant Pepper.* The Beatles.'

'Popular music.'

I nod.

'It's music designed specifically to annoy me. Why is that?'

Doyle says popular music has always annoyed older people. She considers this. 'For once we are in agreement. Goodnight.'

'Goodnight, Ma. Sleep well.'

'I wish.'

We listen to his grandma shuffle through the door and head down the hall. 'She's getting very hard to please, Ma is. For me to please her I would have to be able to recite the names of the kings and queens of England from Alfred the Great to Queen Elizabeth the Second. As she can. I always try to change the subject. And she likes to talk about the DLP. Bores me. She used to be a teacher. At Sodwalls. One room. Fifteen kids. Mum was one of them. I don't think it was much fun. I like debating her when I'm in the mood. I'll deliberately bring up something likely to challenge her. The other day I said, "Why do you bother to pray for my brother to not get called up, when you and Mum and Dad voted for conscription?" It really gave her the shits. Space talk shits her, too. But when she's nice, she's nice. You just don't see it much. I don't, anyway.'

I follow Doyle down into the shop and he grabs a small Coke from the fridge. I do the same. He goes behind the counter of the shop proper and grabs a Mackintosh Rolo chocolate bar and a Small's Club Chocolate for Men. Within a few minutes we are sitting together on the lounge, drinking our Cokes, biting into chocolate and listening to *Sergeant Pepper* on the stereogram.

We look at each other and nod. When it's finished he puts it on again. Some songs are sounding immediately familiar. We love the album cover. The cut-outs. The huge photograph of the four. The uniforms that join the military with art. The concept of The Beatles attending their own funeral. 'They're far more serious than the Fab Four. The Fab Four days are over. That's the significance of the funeral,' says Doyle. 'Something I don't really understand is happening. Dad can see it.'

It's a mood of liberation we can only feel, not articulate.

We talk about how brilliant it all is. 'Fixing a Hole' is Doyle's favourite. I think 'She's Leaving Home' is mine.

'You old sentimentalist,' says Doyle. 'It's Dad's favourite as well.' He talks about his dad's theory that The Beatles have changed music forever. Doyle rustles up a toasted ham, cheese and tomato sandwich with mustard while I look through his record collection and play 'I'm Only Sleeping' from *Revolver*. We agree *Revolver* is a fantastic album. 'Good choice,' he says.

When I get home, I light the fire and wait for Mum. When she gets in, I can tell something's on her mind. She stands warming herself by the fire. 'Roy, I've made a decision. I'm going to divorce your father.' I nod. 'This business of annulment through the church . . . Roy, I've got to be honest, I think it is nonsense. Mr Higgins was at the club tonight. He's a solicitor and he's offered to help me. How do you feel? Your mum would be a divorcee.'

'It doesn't change us at all, Mum. I want whatever you want.'

She kisses me on the forehead. 'Do you want to change schools?'

'Be a Public? No, Mum. I want to stay at De La Salle.'

She nods. I know she's worried that being the son of a divorcee may not allow me to stay at De La Salle. I worry, too. I want to be there with Barbara next year. I want to be with my mates.

•

Sherb is out of hospital. But he's not allowed to teach. We're stuck with Jack Connolly for the rest of the year. Sherb wanders about the school grounds, smoking and watching some of the games being played at lunchtime. Sometimes he sits with the Tropics and Tundra crowd by the toilets and he and Benson smoke together. Twice he's come into our classroom and asked Brother Connor if he can 'borrow' Benson.

'Borrow? Yes, Brother, of course. Borrow? You can have him. Off you go, Benson.'

Together they work on the north garden. And smoke. Benson starts spending all his time with Sherb. We hardly see him in class at all. We agree that Benson has never seemed happier. He whistles while he pushes a wheelbarrow filled with rescued soil from the building site to the garden. He calls Sherb 'Sherbie' openly. 'Where did you want this, Sherbie?'

Sometimes they sit in the new Valiant together. Sherb is teaching him how to drive, which is weird because Sherb doesn't drive at all. And then Sherb starts letting Benson drive the Valiant around the oval. It only happened a couple of times. Brother Hugh put a stop to it. I think Brother Connor complained about the car 'smelling like an ashtray'. But for a small window of time, Benson thought he was King Shit. And he was.

•

Doyle and Dean are called out of class by Brother Hugh. They are to sit for exams set by the Marist Brothers. English and Maths. It's something to do with 'establishing standards', according to Doyle. Dean thought the English was hard, Doyle thought the Maths was hard. Doyle showed me the exam papers. Glad it was him, and not me.

•

Suddenly it's Vocation Week. The school is visited by two priests. They are Franciscans, who wear grey cassocks tied with a thick chord, and sandals, and they're here to talk to any boys who think they might have had 'the calling'. They are going to talk to all of us.

Father Septimus addresses the class. '"And I will make you fishers of men." Who said that? Anyone?'

Brennan puts his hand up. 'Jesus, Father.'

There follows forty minutes of what it's like, what the rewards are of, being a fisher of men. Brewer asks Father Septimus what sort of bait Jesus used.

Father Septimus laughs. 'That is the most interesting question I have ever heard. You are a Jesuit in the making, young man. Our "bait", as you call it, is the truth of Jesus. Jesus himself needed no bait at all. He was simply his perfect self.'

We agree that Father Septimus is pretty boring. Father Paul, his colleague, says almost nothing. He spends his time standing behind Father Septimus, nodding and laughing at jokes that aren't funny that he's clearly heard a thousand times before.

It's a long and boring week. When it came to the interview, I got Father Paul. 'What are your interests?' he asks.

'Playing footy. Playing cricket. Playing tennis. Snooker. Listening to music and watching television.'

'And what part does Jesus play in your life?'

'He's given me the ability to see things many people miss, Father.'

He's intrigued.

'That's very interesting. What like?'

'Like when Jimmy Bannerman gets the ball at dummy half, I know who he's going to pass it to. Like when Ronnie Horner bowls a ball, I know where it's going to go. Stuff like that.'

Father Paul loses interest immediately. He whispers a prayer in Latin and blesses me and I'm allowed to go. Brewer said Father Paul farted when he was talking to him, and it really stunk and they didn't talk about it. We thought Brewer was making this up. Which made us think his story of Father Kane picking his nose in confession during the retreat was made up as well. Priests just didn't do that sort of thing.

Doyle said he spoke to Father Paul about Our Lady. He said he wanted to know why there was such emphasis on her role in the church with so few references to her in the Bible. Doyle quoted Father Paul as saying that 'The Blessed Virgin has made numerous appearances, notably at Fatima. And if you follow your catechism you will find she is the masterwork of God and the start of God bringing mankind into communication with Jesus.' Doyle then asked him if it was okay to pray to Our Lady, to which the answer was yes.

Doyle then pressed him. 'But there is a commandment that says you must not put false gods before God. Isn't Our Lady a false god?'

Father Paul said he would confer with Father Septimus and get back to him. I don't think he did.

The best thing about Vocation Week was that Ray Doyle
was true to his word. I arrived home to find the roof crawling
with men, and an electrician in the house. Mr Croker had let
himself in and was overseeing the work. He was happy to see
me and said he'd heard about my big win in the tennis. He
asked how my dad was getting on and was surprised to learn
that we hadn't heard a word from him for months.

'Not even a letter?'

'No, Sir.'

'So it is just you and your mum?'

'Yes, Sir.'

Then a bloke called Barry Maloney, the electrician, says,
'All good, Mr Croker.'

'Thanks, Barry.' Then he looks at me. 'Well, my boy, let's
see what we can see.' He turns the television on and scrolls
through the channels. There's a bit of a picture. Another bloke,
who I learn is Jim, comes into the room with a big bloke called
Keith and they look at the television. Jim goes back outside
and starts yelling at the other man on the roof. 'Bit to the left,
Barney.' Then Keith shouts at Jim who shouts at Barney.

'Bit more!'

'Bit more!'

'Hold it there!'

'Hold it there!'

Keith fiddles with the tuning at the back of the set and we
have reception! Channel Nine is really clear. So is the ABC.
Keith yells, 'Tie it off there, Jimbo.'

'Tie it off, Barney.'

Barry Maloney leaves, as does the antenna crew. Then Mr Croker leaves, telling me to give Mum his best regards. Mum arrives home from work about ten minutes later. She has a bag of groceries including some mince. One of the girls at work had given her a recipe for savoury mince. I sit her down and we look at *The Huckleberry Hound Show*. Mum has a huge smile on her face. I tell her I think our reception is better than Brewer's or Dean's. The television stays on while Mum cooks and I light the fire. We keep stopping to stare at it. We eat our dinner watching *Voyage to the Bottom of the Sea*. The savoury mince is the finest thing I had ever eaten. Mum was quietly proud of it. Me and Mum had found Heaven here on Earth.

Chapter Eighteen

'Wrap your arms around his feet. You can
smell his boots. There's no sweeter smell.'
FATHER JOHN 'GRASSY' GRANNAL

'Boys, it's all about the ball. Control the
ball and you control the game.'
BROTHER HUGH CORCORAN

The football grand final arrives. As expected, we are
to play Lithgow High School. We have brand-new
jerseys. Deep purple, with two gold V's. And the school crest
in embossed purple and gold over our hearts. Purple socks with
gold hoops. We look a million dollars. We look the business.
I wear a gold number six on my back. O'Brien wears a four.
Flynn twelve. Dean thirteen. Marsland eleven.

Brother Hugh notices, as we warm up, that High School has
included Tank in their team. Tank was playing for Portland.
Brother Hugh raises the issue with Ted Whittaker, the official

who represents the NSW Country Rugby League. Ted agrees that it's a problem. 'No. No. No, you're right there, Mr Brother, a boy can't be registered with two teams in the one competition. Correct.'

The High School coach is Chock Slater. Chock's not a teacher. Chock's not a qualified coach at all. His only qualification is that he's a Slater. Chock is the eldest of the Slater brothers. He is twenty-five. He's been out of prison for three months. Chock Slater is not happy when the objection from Brother Hugh is raised. His first reaction is to say, 'Fuck off, Ted.' But Ted isn't for fucking off. Then Chock draws Ted aside. He speaks to him quietly through gritted teeth. Ted looks terrified. Ted is forty-five. A miner at State Mine Gully. A family of four. He doesn't want to have his legs broken and his car torched. He doesn't want the Slaters as enemies.

'Sorry, Mr Brother, the kid's playing. It's not right, but there's nothing I can do. I'm sorry.'

We're a bit worried. We know what Tank can do. And with Hiscock, Faber and Wilkinson, they have a formidable team. Brother Hugh gets us into a circle and speaks. I don't hear a word he says. I'm formulating a plan.

It's a good crowd. I spot familiar faces in the grandstand. Most of the school is there. Ray Doyle is there. Mum is there with a couple of her theatre group friends. All the Brothers are there. Harold and Jack Connolly. Father Kane and Father Keogh. Father Grannal. Sister Geraldine. Brian Lawson. Herbie

Wilson. Mr Croker and the antenna blokes are there. Sonia. Vicki Westwood. Doyle's there. Benson is standing in front of the grandstand with Sherb. They are both smoking. But it's Barbara I'm looking for.

We wait for the Lithgow town band to finish. They march off to a drumbeat. We run on. There are good cheers. There is support. I look at the hills and remember Brother Michael talking about always having a sense of nature in this place. Nature is looking down upon us. I look at all our familiar mountains. Scotsman's Hill. Mount Walker. Hassans Walls. There is no wind. The spring sun is shining and the blue sky is bluer than any blue I have ever seen. I feel an overwhelming sense of calm. It is a day when Lithgow is the window to wonder.

I have a word with O'Brien before High School kicks off. Flynn catches the ball and passes it to me. I run straight at Tank and chip the ball over his head. I run around him, regather the ball and kick the ball down field. O'Brien, being the fastest player in the state, easily wins the race for the ball and scores under the posts. Flynn converts. Two minutes in and we're up five–nil. They kick off again and Brewer manages to secure the ball, passes it to me and I run again directly at Tank. I shape to kick the ball and he pulls out of the tackle, I run straight by him and have enough speed to confront the High School fullback, John Leggett. O'Brien looms and I shape to pass to him. I don't. Leggett is fooled into covering O'Brien. I score under the posts.

The crowd is stunned. A few car horns blare.

Flynn converts. Ten–nil. They change the way they kick off, and make a shallow kick. It doesn't go the required ten yards and we have a penalty. With his kick, Flynn gets us to their twenty-five yard line. Dean takes the tap and lumbers forward. Flynn at dummy half spins the ball to me. I run at Tank and kick the ball between his legs along the ground into their in-goal area. O'Brien is there to meet the ball and score. Flynn misses with the conversion. Thirteen–nil.

The Catholics in the crowd start to believe. A loud chorus of 'De La Salle! De La Salle! De La Salle!' rings out across the valley.

I notice the High School team is arguing among themselves. Chock Slater is shouting at them. A young policeman talks to him about his language. I hear him shout, 'Fuck yourself, Copper.'

After nearly fifteen minutes, High School finally gets the ball. Faber runs it up and Dean and Marsland, working as one, bring him to ground. I decide that under no circumstances is Tank to get the ball. It's obvious to me who is going to get the ball to him and I sit on Bannerman and hammer him each time he gets the ball. I have eyes on no one else. At one stage Bannerman stays down after a good tackle, pretending to be knocked out. Milking a penalty. There are boos. The game is stopped while the St John's Ambulance men attend to him. Chock Slater leads a 'Send him off!' chant. It gains traction from the Publics in the crowd. 'Send him off! Send him off!'

The referee, from Cowra, calls me out. 'Number six.' I think I'm in trouble and walk over to him.

'Son, I'm going to penalise you, but you haven't done anything wrong. I want to leave here in one piece, you understand?' I nod. They get a penalty.

They are now inside our twenty-five yard line. It's a set piece and I can see exactly what is going to happen. I talk to O'Brien. Play begins and instead of heading towards Bannerman, I run at Tank and intercept the ball from Bannerman that is meant for him. I have broken the line and O'Brien is beside me. I pass him the ball and he's away. I've never seen him accelerate with such driven, passionate, blinding, God-given speed. I was at full pace yet felt like I was standing still. No man in all of the history of the world could have caught O'Brien on that sublime Lithgow day. The golden number four leaves us all in his wake. He is in again under the posts. High School hang their heads. Chock has screamed himself hoarse.

Half-time. Eighteen–nil. The Lithgow town band is back. We stand in a cluster by the sideline. We eat oranges. We can't use the dressing rooms because the under twenty-ones are getting ready. Father Grannal strolls over and has a word to Flynn before offering some advice to Dean and Marsland. I sit on the grass and scour the grandstand for Barbara.

She's there! My Barbara is here. She's right against the fence. She is again with Deirdre and the netball girl whose name I don't know. I ask Flynn if he knows her. 'Eh?' is his response. His head is in the game. And fair enough.

Brother Hugh walks amongst us. He is a reassuring presence. He touches a few of the blokes on the head and nods.

He hunkers down beside me. 'Keep playing like Roy Slaven,' he quietly says to me. He pats me on the back. He quietly says something to O'Brien and moves on. O'Brien and I look at each other. He grins. We're enjoying ourselves.

We kick off. Tank gets the ball. He winds up. Flynn dives at his feet and collects both of them sweetly between his arms. Tank falls on the ball he holds and is winded. The game is held up. There will be a scrum as Tank had lost control of the ball.

I pat Flynn on the back for a great tackle. He says, 'It's Pat. Pat from Wallerawang. With Barbara and Deirdre.'

'Okay. Thanks. Is she a Catholic?'

'Oh, fuck, yeah.'

I knew Flynn would know.

We win the scrum. The ball comes to me and I throw a thirty-foot torpedo pass that flies like a bullet, hoping to find O'Brien. O'Brien finds it. He's away. Again! Under the posts. For some reason I can do nothing wrong. Nor can O'Brien. We can hardly hear ourselves speak, such is the roar from the crowd and the blare of car horns. I look at the grandstand and hats and things are being hurled into the air like confetti.

O'Brien finishes the game with eight tries. A record. I scored three and Dean barged over late in the game off a sweet little pass from Flynn that fooled everyone. Including Dean. The final score was fifty-two to nil. The High School team grudgingly shake hands with us and they slope off. We stand as a team in a circle, Brother Hugh in the middle. We say a Hail Mary together.

I'm keen to shower and get changed and see Barbara but Brother Hugh takes me and O'Brien aside and says Ron Livermore wants to speak with us. He's the under eighteens state selector.

He's about fifty years old. Solid. Still fit. His suit fits. He thanks Brother Hugh and looks at us. 'I know Rugby League. I've been watching it all my life. I don't think I've ever seen what you boys did today.' He looks about. People are readying themselves for the under twenty-one final. He puts his index finger on O'Brien's chest. 'You'll be playing for New South Wales.' He pokes his finger into my chest. 'You scare me, son. You're going to be a legend.' He shakes my hand. 'One day I can tell my grandkids that I shook the hand of Roy Slaven. I've spoken to your mother. You're Baz Slaven's nephew, aren't you?'

'Yes, Sir.'

Chock Slater has got himself into a fight and is arrested. He's frogmarched towards a paddy wagon. He screams obscenities. It's quite hard to work out what he is saying. His voice has gone. 'Fuck'n pigs! You stink! Stink. Pigs stink!' I think is what he's saying. A crowd surrounds him shouting 'loser' and 'arsehole' and the paddy wagon is bashed and rocked with angry hands as he's hoisted unwillingly into the back. The paddy wagon moves off to the sound of car horns.

The under twenty-one match starts. We shower, dress, and I meet up with Mum and her friends, Kathy Wilson and Bev Achurch. We go to Tony's Coffee Lounge in Main Street. I have a chocolate milkshake and Mum and her friends have cappuccinos. The talk turns quickly to *The Boy Friend*. Bev Achurch is in the chorus and Kathy Wilson is the lead, Polly. Mum is to be Fay, as predicted by Tony Doyle. While I'm sort of interested, my thoughts are really elsewhere. I ask Mum if I can go.

'Of course, darling,' She stands and kisses me on the forehead and whispers, 'I'm so proud of you.'

I ride out to O'Brien's place in Macaulay Street. Flynn is there. Mr O'Brien had been at the match. He thinks we could have beaten any team in the world the way we played today. He thinks Brother Hugh is a 'master coach'.

O'Brien and Flynn and I laze about in the backyard by the chook pen. The air is thick with the perfume of the honeysuckle that grows wild up the wall of the leaning timber garage. We go through some of the moments of the game. O'Brien said all he had to do was run into the gaps and the ball was there for him. Flynn said he thought Dean and Marsland, again, were the unsung heroes. 'They didn't take a backwards step.' We talk of ways we could improve. We wonder if it could possibly be true that we could be playing for New South Wales next year. Ron Livermore had told Flynn he was impressed with him. We ponder what might become of Chock Slater. O'Brien wonders, 'What is it with Publics?'

Flynn's going to the pictures with Vicki Westwood. Brewer had agreed to fill in for him at *The Clarion* delivering papers. O'Brien and Sonia are going as well. I tell them I have no Barbara news. I won't be at the pictures.

I have a night at home by myself watching television in my pyjamas. I fall asleep in front of a Humphrey Bogart film. Mum wakes me when she gets in from the RSL Club. On the television is nothing but the test pattern. I only half wake up and go straight to bed and sleep the sleep of the dead. Mum turns the television off.

•

At the Monday morning school assembly Brother Hugh asks for the football team to come to the front. He has the competition trophy, which he gives to Flynn, the captain, and Flynn holds it aloft and Brother Hugh calls for three rousing cheers and we all feel very proud. He then goes on to tell the school what it already knows – the historic nature of the score and the bold style of play, and what it means to the school and how proud all of us should be, and we lower our heads for an Our Father as a prayer of thanks. Sherb and Benson watch the assembly from the garden. They both lean against their long-handled shovels.

Chapter Nineteen

'Never felt closer to God, Dean. Saint
Joseph is looking after me today.'
BROTHER HUBERT

'This is God playing with us, boys. Our
confusion must give Him pleasure.'
BROTHER HUBERT

It's a Geography class. Harold is stressing the importance of lucerne as a cash crop, based on observations made on his drive to Bathurst on the weekend. He then launches into Christaller's theory of industrial location. 'It's the relationship between raw materials, labour and markets, boys. Look at what has happened here in Lithgow with the smelting of iron ore. It became too expensive to transport the iron ore to Lithgow. Much cheaper to transport the coal to the coast and smelt the iron near a port.'

Benson runs into the classroom. 'Sir. Sherb's fallen over. In the garden.'

We scramble out of the classroom, Harold and Dean in the lead. We find Sherb lying on his face under a flowering camellia. A shovel is by his side. A magpie sits in the middle of his back acting as a defiant guardian.

Harold rolls him over and puts his ear to his mouth.

'He's still breathing. Doyle, run in and telephone the hospital.'

Doyle heads off.

'Stand back, boys. Well back.'

Benson sits on the ground beside Sherb, holding his hand. He's in tears, saying, 'Don't leave me, Sherbie. Don't leave me. Please don't leave me.'

Brother Hugh, Brother Michael and Brother Connor join us. We say a decade of the rosary. Harold sits on the lawn with his hand on Sherb's shoulder. Benson rubs the hand he holds. The ambulance arrives and Sherb is carried to it on a stretcher. Brother Hugh holds Benson by the shoulders and says, 'Go with him.'

Benson says, 'Thanks, Brother,' and he clambers in beside the old dying man, gently takes his hand as the doors of the ambulance are closed and it slowly glides off.

•

After school, Dean, Doyle and me ride up to the hospital. Mrs Dean is there. She says Sherb can't have any visitors and it doesn't look good at all. But she relents and says, 'Okay, just a few minutes.' Sherb is in a one-bed room. He has a mask over his face delivering oxygen and various wires are attached to his chest. A machine makes beeping noises. Benson is still with him, his total focus on Sherb's open but sightless eyes.

'Can he hear us?' I whisper.

'I don't know,' says Benson, who is eating some thick soup provided by Mrs Dean.

We're standing there in silence, watching Sherb breathe, and Mrs Dean pokes her head in and says we'd better go. She says the doctor is certain Sherb will make it through the night. Benson asks if he's got to go, too. 'I think it's best,' she says. Dean offers to double him home on his bike. And he does.

Doyle rides with me back to my place. I show him the new television set. He's very impressed with the reception. I show him the new washing machine. He's not all that interested but pretends to be. He says he's got to go. We have exams coming up.

We share a sense of emptiness. We know we'll never see Sherb at school again. Or hear him recite poetry. Or walk with him in the sun by the river and be shown the glorious wonders we cannot see by ourselves.

•

Jack Connolly gives us back our marked test papers on *Great Expectations*. Thanks to Doyle's help, I get sixty-seven per cent, the highest mark I've ever got in English. Brewer sees my mark and rolls his eyes in both disbelief and disappointment. I'd let the Tundra down. Brennan manages to get a minus mark. He'd littered his answers with obscenities, gambling that Jack

Connolly wouldn't bother to read his paper. He read us a couple of his answers down by the toilets at lunchtime.

'Pip's problem is that he's a fat little poof who gets a stiffy whenever Miss Havisham farts', was one.

'Mr Jaggers washes his hands all the time because he can't stop beating his old fellow under the desk, like Benson', is another.

Brewer is in tears of laughter and says they're the best answers he's ever heard. 'I'd have given you one hundred per cent, Brenno. That is just too good.'

•

Mum's out rehearsing three nights a week. And she's making some dresses for the production. She sings 'Won't You Charleston With Me' while she sews. She has a spring in her step. She practises dance moves in the lounge room in front of the television when the ads are on. She doesn't realise the ads are the most entertaining parts of most shows.

Mum has had a couple of meetings with Mr Higgins regarding the divorce. She has to prove Dad's done something wrong. Mr Higgins isn't sure Dad throwing one or two punches over the course of sixteen years is enough. The fact that he's left us high and dry is apparently 'compelling', but Mum feels she's being forced into 'making things up'. She is refusing to make things up. She doesn't want Dad to gain a reputation worse than it currently is, which, to be fair, isn't great. She is hoping the 'We don't love each other anymore' argument might be enough. Mr Higgins doesn't think it is. And Dad hasn't responded to any correspondence sent to him by Mr Higgins, and Mr Higgins isn't sure that the address he's been sending his letters is correct. Or current. Or whether Dad has left any forwarding address, given it's unlikely he'd still be shearing in Caragabal.

Mum's determined it's not going to spoil her theatre experience. 'It's so thrilling, Roy. There are no secrets. We talk about everything. There is nothing taboo. You should hear what some of them come out with. So shameless. There is no shame in doing anything. Mr Davies says the theatre is a moral-free zone. "We should explore every nuance of life in order to be able to find it in performance." Honestly. The church would hate the theatre. Kathy Wilson calls the theatre "The Church of Life".'

•

Death arrived for Brother Hubert at a quarter past ten on October the twenty-eighth. Benson was with him. While his eyes were open, he never really woke up. Mrs Dean said the doctor thought it was a stroke as well as a heart attack.

Mrs Dean said she asked Benson to close his eyes for the last time. 'Nearly broke his little heart. I got the ambulance to take him home.' She pointed out that Sherb had been called to Heaven on the feast day of Saint Jude, 'Hope of the Hopeless', and that she and Mr Dean were looking into 'a solution' for Benson.

We learnt of Sherb's death during Maths. Brother Connor broke the news to us after receiving a whispered message from

Brother Hugh. The classroom went silent. Many were in tears. I was. Doyle was. Dean was. Brewer was. Flynn was. Brennan was. O'Brien was. Our whole small world was. And made so much smaller without Sherb.

Brother Connor sat at the front desk and put his hands over his face to gather composure. He took out his rosary beads. He prayed silently. We all did.

The two schools, Saint Patrick's and De La Salle, formed a guard of honour that stretched all the way down Hospital Hill. Old Boys still living in the town swelled the numbers. A black hearse slowly made its way out of the hospital gates and glided slowly down the street. Everybody waved. There were cries of 'Bye, Sherb!' 'Thanks, Sherb!' 'Bot a fag from Saint Peter, Sherb!' 'See you, mate.' 'Travel safely, Sherb!' The hearse rounded the corner into Mort Street on its journey to Oakhill College at Castle Hill where Nature's gentle man was to be buried after a small private service.

I turn away and suddenly Barbara is standing beside me. She hands me a fresh handkerchief and I dry my eyes and blow my nose. I start to give it back to her, but instead fold it and put it in my pocket.

'Am I allowed to talk to you?'

'Yes.'

'Thank you,' I say.

And the emotion sort of gets to me. I heave with grief. Barbara rubs my shoulder. Her handkerchief is used again. I compose myself, grab my bike and walk her home. At one point, we hold hands. She says her dad's attitude towards me was changing. The tennis match helped. He didn't think much of Brian Lawson. We agree we'll go to the pictures when the exams are over.

I ride home, showing off, seeing how far I can go with my hands off the handlebars. I sing, 'All You Need Is Love'. I'm convinced it's possible that, with Barbara's father, Sherb has interceded on my behalf in Heaven, where he undoubtedly would be.

•

The 'solution' Mr and Mrs Dean found on the feast day of Saint Jude, Hope of the Hopeless, was to visit the school that night and talk to Brother Hugh about Benson. They argued that Benson should be employed at the school as a caretaker to maintain the gardens and do general dogsbody work. Brother Hugh immediately telephoned Mr Austin who agreed to sponsor Benson but wanted no publicity. Brother Hugh was effusive with his thanks to Mr Austin and the next day Benson left school and stayed at the school. He gave Doyle and me a private tour of the north garden, which was strictly out of bounds. 'Sherb wanted petunias in this bed. And he wanted a veggie garden. Not here but over where the blackberry bushes are.'

Then he sees a First Former. 'Hey! Where do you think you're going? Go around the other way. This is strictly out of bounds. You understand?'

'Yes, Sir.'

Doyle asked him what the new Valiant was like to drive. 'It's a bit stiff changing from first to second gear. Haven't tried second to third.'

•

Someone at the theatre group puts Mum onto Scott's Heat 'n' Eat TV dinners, available at Woolworths. We have them three nights a week. Roast lamb and the fricassee of chicken are our favourites by miles. Mum says they have saved her life. She hates cooking more than anything in the world. 'Cooking makes me sick,' I heard her telling Kathy Wilson. 'Roy never complains, God bless him. Used to drive Bob mad. I played with the boys all the time, never learnt to cook.'

Mum was getting quite thick with the theatre group. She went to their awards night where Kathy Wilson won an award for her performance in *Ass and Philosophers*. Mum even started bringing plays home to read. *The One Day of the Year* was one. *Summer of the Seventeenth Doll* was another. And *The Boy Friend* was having a dress rehearsal. She had finished making what she called 'the flapper dresses' and the director, Mr Davies, was very pleased with them. 'He's worried they'll steal the show. Such a nice man.'

•

Exam week arrives. Dean and Doyle take it very seriously. The Tropics are as one in this matter. The Temperates take it pretty seriously as well, and the Tundras find it all boring. I'm kicking myself that I haven't really prepared at all. We sit in the room Mr Goggin says will be the library next year. Mr Goggin will be building the shelves. We have a desk each. The work I did with Doyle helps me a lot in English and I find I can at least try to answer most of the questions. Usually I leave most answers blank. For the first time in my life I run out of time. Brewer and Brennan and Hall finished their papers after about ten minutes. Brewer said I looked like a crawler. I did look like a crawler. But I actually felt good.

I struggled through Maths, but got all the trigonometry questions right. I think. Geography was mostly the stuff Harold had been cramming into us over the last couple of weeks. I remembered the Christaller stuff. Science? I don't think Brother Michael would be that happy, but the good thing was, it was all multiple choice so I had a one in four chance with all of them.

History was the last exam. I listened to Dean and Doyle talking about it at lunchtime, before we went in.

'Sarajevo was just a spark. Not a cause. The cause was Nationalism.'

Dean agrees. 'And alliances.'

Doyle agrees. 'It'll be the first question.'

Dean says, 'There'll be a question about Aboriginal migration.'

'Yes,' says Doyle, 'There were three waves. Negritos?'

'Correct.'

'Murrayans.'

'And?'

'Carpentarians.'

'Full marks.'

'At least three thousand years ago.'

Dean and Doyle had their heads filled with this stuff. Stuff that would never be needed or of any use to anyone anywhere, anytime.

Whatever the subject, whatever the problem, they would either know, or if they didn't know, they knew how to find the answers. And they enjoyed finding the answers. Doyle had a *Book of General Knowledge* he made good use of.

Also, Doyle's beer room had a set of *Time/Life* books his father subscribed to. He said one came every month. They sat on the top row of the four-box high DA wall, which stretched from one side of the room to the other. The layout of Doyle's beer room changed all the time, depending on the number of boxes. Some of the books were all about the natural world. Some about 'The Greeks', 'The Romans', 'The Incas', 'The Universe', 'Michelangelo', 'Leonardo'. Name a subject, Doyle could find something with great pictures and illustrations.

And he liked a magazine that I hated. *Mad* magazine. He said his brother got it for him at the factory where he worked as a fitter and turner. It was his day job. He knew a bloke who got them in Sydney. You couldn't buy the magazine in Lithgow. 'Dad hates it. He's banned it from the house. He says it's dangerous. I think it's unbelievably good. It only makes sense if you watch television. It sends up everything. Nothing is sacred. I hide it behind the Bible in the lounge room.'

He lent it to me but it wasn't funny to me at all. It gave me the shits. I didn't let Mum see it. I don't know why. It wasn't dirty. It was just unsettling. You needed to be weird to find it funny. I didn't want Mum worrying that I was weird. And I wasn't. I didn't like it. I gave it back to him. At school.

'What's that?' Brother Connor saw me pass Doyle the magazine.

Doyle holds it up. '*Mad* magazine, Brother.'

'What magazine?'

'*Mad*, Brother.'

Brother Connor takes it and flicks through it. He stops at certain pages. 'Doyle, is this yours? Or Slaven's?'

'I borrowed it, Brother. From a friend of my brother's. I lent it to Slaven.' Brother Connor kept flicking and stopping from time to time. He looks carefully at Doyle. 'Doyle, this kind of thing isn't fit for a normal mind.'

'I know, Brother.'

'You have me flummoxed here, Doyle. I don't know whether this should be reported or not.'

He returns to a page. 'This, for example, makes the American soldiers in Vietnam look ridiculous.'

'It's a view, Brother.'

'Not a view I like, Doyle. Not a view I like at all.' He looks at another page. 'Who is Gilligan?'

'*Gilligan's Island*, Brother. It's a show on television.'

'And Gilligan is the President of the United States here. The point being?'

'The point being that Gilligan, being a bumbling sort of idiot, would be doing just as good a job as President Johnson, Brother.'

'Yes. Yes. Yes, I see. I don't like any of this at all, Doyle. It's subversive. And I don't want it on the school grounds. Understood?'

'Yes, Brother.'

Doyle put it in his port.

'Do your parents know you are looking at this?'

'Dad does, Brother.'

'And he approves?'

'He hates it, Brother.'

'Good. So do I. Makes me feel like I need a bath.'

Dean had the full set of *The Encyclopaedia Britannica*. And the full set of Biggles. And Billy Bunter books. It was a weird family. One night I was there, Dean and his three brothers and his mum and dad are sitting at the dining table all working on homework. The radio isn't on. The television isn't on. It's just work and whispers. The television isn't allowed on until all homework is finished. Dean finishes last and we almost miss the start of *Peyton Place*.

I needed the radio on to do homework. So did Doyle. He often spent time in his mum and dad's Valiant, in the backyard, with his AWA transistor radio on. Or he'd be in his grandma's flat at the back of the house. I called Doyle's house the 'House of Doors'. My theory is that Doyle needed a lot of doors and the sound of the radio to block out the screaming that came from his sister. He said it was getting worse. He now wore a scar just above his left eye where his sister had hit him with a fork. She threw it while they were having dinner. He sometimes sat in the car with her for hours while she writhed and screamed in the back seat. 'It gives Mum a break.'

We got our exam results. Dean came first in the class, eight marks ahead of Doyle. Lennan came third. Dean was first in Maths, Science and Commerce. Doyle was first in English and Geography and Religious Knowledge. I passed. Jack Connolly said he should be considered for the Teacher of the Year Award on the strength of me coming twelfth in English. I passed everything. Fifty-one per cent in Science! Pretty good in History. Nailed the Aboriginal migration question and argued Sarajevo was 'just the spark'.

Mum couldn't believe it when I told her. 'You passed? Everything?' Then she had a funny look on her face. 'I swore I would never tell you this. Kathy Wilson thinks you might be the perfect man.'

I didn't know how to react.

'Mind you, she'd had a few drinks and wasn't making much sense at all at the time.' She smiled. 'I think she's right, though.' Then she laughed and kissed me on the forehead.

Chapter Twenty

'This file is a flat bastard, boys. Don't
be scared of the word.'
JACK CONNOLLY

'As soon as a boy goes to the public
school, he loses his faith. Fact.'
FATHER JIM KEOGH

I spoke to Flynn about the pictures on Saturday night. He said he couldn't go but he'd ask Deirdre to speak with Barbara. Flynn knows every girl in Lithgow. Knows the networks, the alliances, the gossip. Dean thinks he will end up a diplomat. Or a spy. Pretty late in the week he tells me Barbara is good for the pictures and she'll meet me out the front of the Theatre Royal Café. This is good news.

I shave with the razor Dad left behind. It's as blunt as buggery, but I muddle through. I'm reminded of Sherb as I do it. I put some Tabac aftershave on. It had been given to Dad by someone and had never been used. Mum probably gave it to him. I wear my corduroys and my best shirt. I polish my school shoes. I don't have a long mirror to see the total effect. I leave the house and walk to the Royal.

I cut through Queen Elizabeth Park and I can see Barbara waiting for me. She stands alone in a crowd outside the café. She's wearing a sleeveless dress with a bird pattern on it, and plain black shoes. Her hair is up. A blue folded jumper rests over her arm. I cross the street and she sees me and shakes her head as she smiles. She's passed her exams as well. We talk about us being in the same class next year when our schools unite.

Some people recognise me from the tennis match. 'Well done, mate.'

We go in. She insists on paying for her own ticket. We're back under the dress circle. The film is *Camelot*. It's not really my sort of film, but Barbara really gets into it. I find myself looking at Barbara and she looks at me. We hold hands. Towards the end she is in tears. I have her handkerchief in my pocket. Mum had washed and ironed it for me. I give it to her and she is grateful.

The café is closed. I walk her home. We stand in the street. I hold both her hands. I lean forward awkwardly and I am aware of her breath. We kiss. Me and Barbara. In Main Street. Kissing. She shivers.

'I forgot I have a jumper.'

'Can we do this again?'

'Yes. I'd like that.'

I walk off and when I turn back she's still standing on the footpath watching me. I should have gone back and cuddled her again. I wanted to. I think she wanted me to. But instead I waved and strode off. I see Harold sitting alone in his Volkswagen by the park. I don't acknowledge him at all. I pretend I don't see him. Afterwards, I was worried he might have thought I was being rude. His car is so obvious.

·

School is a lot more relaxed with the exams over. Brother Hugh talks to us about what next year will look like with the Saint Patrick's girls joining us. 'They can be a fearful distraction, boys. Some of you will be inclined to show off. Bear in mind what happened to Adam in the Garden of Eden. The history of humankind is littered with men who have fallen for the wiles of a woman, boys. You must be strong. Don't be tempted. Pray for strength.'

After school I meet up with Doyle at the Railway Institute and we had a frame of snooker. I tell him all about my night with Barbara and how great it's going to be having her in our class next year. 'I wonder if I'll be allowed to sit with her.'

Doyle doesn't think we'll be allowed to sit with them. 'We'll have single desks. Like we used in the exams. That's what Brother Michael said.'

'Who would you like to sit with, Doyle?'

'I have loved Carmel since the first day of kindergarten. There is no one else. There's never been anyone else. Susan Morgan for a few weeks but I have remained steadfast and loyal in the hope that, someday, something might happen.'

This surprised me. Carmel would sometimes come to the pool and she and Doyle would snipe at each other. I thought she gave him the shits.

'The problem is, though, I just give her the shits. I can't help myself. I try to impress her by being smart. I've spoken to Flynn about it. He doesn't like her all that much. He thinks she's up herself. And she probably is a bit. He said to just stop trying to give her the shits. Easier said than done. But. We sort of enjoy shitting each other. I think. I love it when I give her the shits. I'm not sure she loves it so much. I dunno. I just don't know. I can't train myself to be myself, because I don't know who myself is. I don't when I'm with Carmel anyway. "Broads, you can't live with them, can't live without them."' Then he sings 'You're Going to Lose That Girl' and I sing the counter melody.

I let Doyle pot the black. I'd set it up three times for him. He enjoyed the win.

He told no one he'd beaten me. Because he knew I had let him win.

•

We're painting the Science room on Sunday afternoon. Sister Geraldine is in charge. Doyle thinks she enjoys the company of us boys. She seems to. There's me and Dean and Doyle and O'Brien. O'Brien is to be school captain next year.

Dean and Doyle are to be house captains along with Lennan and Marsland. The Brothers have made the decision. There's no vote.

Dean takes charge of the painting. He's the only one with experience. Sister Geraldine helps us lay the drop sheets and, before long, a wall is completed. It's a sort of light green. Dean does what he calls 'cutting in' and the rest of us fill it in. Sister Geraldine watches. She can't really paint dressed in her full habit. Doyle asks her how hot she gets in summer. She argues that the habit actually has a cooling effect in summer. Doyle doesn't believe her. 'Sounds like wishful thinking, Sister.'

Dean points out that Bedouins wear dark heavy clothing in the heat of the desert because it traps the perspiration and has a cooling effect.

'Is it a Middle Eastern design, Sister?' Doyle wants to know.

Dean says, 'Could be North African.'

'Mother Mary MacKillop designed them.'

We're none the wiser, really.

Sister Geraldine disappears for a while, to later return with a plate of tomato sandwiches. She likes the work we're doing.

'Are you allowed to listen to the radio?' Doyle again.

'We don't.'

'What about television?'

'No. No television.'

'So you've never heard The Beatles?'

'I can live without having heard The Beatles.'

'Is Sister Francis allowed to play her guitar in the convent?'

'At times, yes.'

'So what's the difference between listening to Sister Francis and listening to the radio?'

She smiles. 'Listening to Sister Francis and her guitar is an act of penance.'

Doyle laughs. Sister Geraldine laughs. And blushes. Sister Geraldine has a soft spot for Doyle. 'You're trying to get me into trouble.'

Brother Hugh blunders in. He doesn't see Sister Geraldine at first. 'Fine job you're doing here, boys.' Then he sees her. 'Gnnrrgh, hunnngggrrgh, Sister, gnnrrgh.' And his face turns red and he backs out of the room. We all look at each other. Sister Geraldine has her eyes closed as if offering up a silent prayer, which she probably was.

We roll up the drop sheets. The Science room looks proud.

•

The Boy Friend is about to open. Mum says she has two free tickets. I ask her if I could ask Barbara.

'I'd like to meet her.'

So the next day I ask Flynn to speak to Deirdre to ask Barbara if she'd be allowed to come with me. He's happy to do this and gets back to me the next day. It's all good.

Opening night. Mum is a nervous wreck. I tell her how beautiful she looks and wish her luck. She does look beautiful. I kiss her on the forehead. Kathy Wilson picks her up and I walk into town.

Barbara is waiting for me outside her place in Main Street. We look at each other and realise we are both dressed exactly as we were when we went to the pictures. We think it's a good sign. We walk down the end of Main Street to the Trades Hall. There's a good crowd. Full house. The talk is loud. Everyone is talking. Some are shouting. There are shrieks of laughter. We have great seats five rows back from the front and in the middle. I look around. I know no one. Most people seem to know each other. I whisper to Barbara that we appear to be the only Catholics here. Then the hall goes dark and silent and the curtains part.

There's so much to look at. So much going on. Some titters from the crowd at something I've missed. I only have eyes for Fay. Fay is great. Kathy Wilson is Polly Browne and she is very good. Julian Sheahan is the leading man and he's just as good. It is really very professional. Everyone knows the lines and the singing is confident. I could see Mr Davies's point about the flappers' dresses. They were the most exciting costumes by far. Polly sometimes had to fight for attention. She looked a bit plain when the lights were really bright.

We watch people mingling at half-time. Some women are dressed to the nines. A lot of people are congratulating a bloke I take to be Mr Davies. 'Marvellous, Des. Simply marvellous.'

'I'd forgotten how strong the music is.'

'Pity you can't tour this, Des.'

'Triumph, Des.'

Some of the men are wearing cravats. Barbara told me what they were. I'd never heard of a cravat. Barbara thinks it's a very odd crowd and I see what she means. There is a lot of gesturing and some men are calling other men 'darling'. 'Darling, I was cut to the quick.' And some men are referring to other men as 'she'. 'Oh, she's a fine one to talk.'

Barbara and me are ducks out of water. Barbara thought the half-time show was as good as the show itself. I didn't disagree. It wasn't anything like the mass crowd or the football crowd.

The second half is just as strong. During 'Poor Little Pierrette' I look at Barbara and she is glowing, transported by the melody. We stand with the crowd at the conclusion. There are cheers and whistles. The pianist is presented with flowers by a woman dressed in black. Then Kathy Wilson is presented with flowers. Julian Sheahan is presented with what appears to be a small box of cigars. Then Des Davies takes to the stage and, when the applause dies down, he tells people refreshments are available upstairs at the Court House Hotel across the street.

We wait outside for Mum. After about twenty minutes she appears with Kathy Wilson and Julian Sheahan. Mum has been given flowers too. Julian calls me 'the sporting savant'.

I introduce Barbara to Mum. Mum gives her a cuddle. 'Lovely to meet you, Barbara.' Then she stands back. 'Well? What did you think?'

'Best show I've ever seen,' I say.

Mum says to the others, 'It's the only show he's ever seen.'

I can tell they want to get going, so I say that we'll leave them to the celebrations. Barbara and I are too young to go into the hotel.

'I'll catch you at home, darling. Don't wait up for me. Lovely to meet you, Barbara.' Then she stops and says to Barbara, 'Are you a size ten?' She nods. 'I've got a beautiful fabric that would suit you down to the ground. Leave it with me.'

'Come on, Paulette!' And Mum darts across the street and is swallowed by cravats and squeals and glasses of champagne.

Barbara says she likes my mum. 'She is so young'. I tell her about the prospect of divorcing Dad. 'How old was she when she was married?'

'Seventeen. She was sixteen when it got serious. By serious, I mean I was on the way. She talked to Father Keogh about annulment, but it's too expensive and was going to take forever.' We walk down Main Street. We notice a poster. Normie Rowe is coming to Lithgow with his band The Playboys. Barbara was unsure about Normie Rowe. 'It Ain't Necessarily So' was banned by the Catholic station 2SM and was the subject of a particularly fiery sermon from Father Keogh. Normie Rowe was seen as anti-Catholic. She said Flynn was going to go with Vicki Westwood, but she was not allowed. We arrive at her place. Again, we kiss. And I hold her. Our breathing is short. 'Can we do this again?'

'Yes.'

Another kiss. A really long one. Our tongues touch for the smallest moment. We look closely at each other. She turns. I watch her go in.

I walk home. 'Poor Little Pierrette' burns into my brain, like one of the *Camelot* songs did. It's not cold so I don't light the fire. The television just has the test pattern. The radio is playing something really old and boring. I feel wired. I force myself to bed and lie there thinking of Barbara. And she and I sing 'Poor Little Pierrette' together. The lullaby eventually works. I don't hear Mum get home.

•

Mum doesn't get out of bed until one o'clock the next day. She's wearing her dressing-gown and she's cold. I'd been up to Dean's for breakfast. I'd seen Mrs Dean when I was doing laps of the Main Street on my bike hoping to see Barbara. Mrs Dean insisted I join them for breakfast when I told her I hadn't had mine yet. So glad she did. Scrambled eggs with crisp bacon. First time I'd had scrambled eggs. I asked Mrs Dean how they're made and she showed me.

Mum isn't interested in what the Deans had had for breakfast. She is cold. I grab some paper and sticks and get the fire going. I should have lit the fire before I went out. Mum is sitting with a hot water bottle. I ask her if she'd like a cup of tea. 'Oh, please, yes. Thank you.' I was going to make scrambled eggs for her, but we had no milk. Instead, I boil an egg and make her some toast. The fire is starting to crackle and I throw some coal on it and the heat arrives. It lifts Mum's spirits.

'I got in at six. It was light. It's never happened before. Oh, Roy, it was such a party. It was after midnight when Tony Doyle and his band turned up. They played just for us. We danced. We laughed. Did you enjoy it?'

'It was fantastic, Mum.'

'Did Barbara enjoy it?'

'She did.'

'She seems a lovely girl, Roy.'

'She is, Mum. She thought it was a strange crowd.'

'Strange? I suppose they are. They're theatre people, Roy. They're wonderful. They are happy being themselves.'

I don't know what she means and let it go. It makes me think of Doyle not knowing who he was when he was with Carmel. I didn't know what he meant, just pretended I did.

Mum stares at the fire. I see to her boiled egg. I place it on a plate beside a thick slice of buttered toast. She asks me to get her a knife. She peels the egg and slices it onto the toast. Then cuts the bread into bite-sized pieces. 'This is just the best thing anyone could have made me. Thank you.' Then she looks at me. 'Sit down with me, love.' I do. 'Barbara is your girlfriend.' I nod, because she sort of is. But it wasn't official like Flynn and Vicki Westwood or O'Brien and Sonia.

'Girls at your age sometimes want to show their boyfriends how much they love them. And sometimes boys get very

excited. And determined. And before you know it, you are
. . . being intimate with one another.'

I don't know where to look. She's talking about rooting.
There's a fair bit of silence, then, 'I don't want you to make
the mistake your father did. And I don't want Barbara to
make the mistake I did. I don't regret having had you, my
darling. Not at all. You know that. I've always told you that.
I just want you and Barbara to be very careful. There can be
consequences for passion. Do you understand me?' I nod.

Mum goes on. 'If, down the track, and I mean, well down
the track, you need protection, you won't find it at Dougherty's.
Go to the top chemist.'

I realise that Mum's talking about 'frenchies'. We sit quietly.
Mum finishes her egg. Eventually I say, 'Mum, isn't what you're
talking about sinful?'

'Sinful? Whether it's sinful or not is beside the point. It's
human nature, love. The church is so impractical. So unrealistic.
Sometimes the church is just wrong. Those priests are not living
in the real world. And the Brothers? Mad. All of them have
absolutely no idea of what it's like to be a woman in a world
made by men for men.'

I realised Mum was more concerned about Barbara than me.

Mum runs herself a bath. She's got another performance
of *The Boy Friend* tonight. I put the radio on and wash the
dishes. My mind is reeling. Does Mum really think I should
buy frenchies? When Hall was caught with a frenchie at school
it was a total scandal. He was nearly expelled and his parents

had to come to the school from Wallerawang. I can't imagine ever walking into the top chemist and asking for a frenchie.

•

I ride back into town and cruise up Main Street on the off-chance Barbara might be about. She's not. I call into the café beside the picture theatre. Brewer is there playing pinball by himself. He tells me he's thinking of leaving school at the end of the year. He didn't do so well in the exams and doesn't want to have to repeat. He is a year older than me. He says he's been offered work as an apprentice spray-painter with Billy Coleman at the panelbeaters. He thinks Brennan might be leaving as well. Hall is leaving. He's working with his dad as an apprentice builder. Mahon is going as well. He doesn't know what Mahon is going to do. The Temperate and Tundra are starting to look a bit thin.

While I'm talking to Brewer, Doyle calls in. He said he was just having a ride and looking for something to do. We leave Brewer to it, because he hasn't got his bike, and cruise over to the netball courts where two games are happening. All teams are Publics, so we move on. As we're about to ride off, a carload of Slaters arrives. They park by a court. The four get out. They each have a longneck bottle of beer. They slouch against the car bonnet and have a guzzle and a gaze at the games.

We ride out to O'Brien's. He's working with his dad in the vegetable garden. Mr O'Brien grills me on what sport interests me the most. 'All of them,' I say. He says I might need a manager. Doyle tells him he's my manager.

'I've got big plans for Roy, Mr O'Brien. He's going to play for Australia in cricket, tennis and Rugby League and he's going to put on snooker demonstrations in the clubs. He's going to be in high demand.'

Mr O'Brien is very impressed. 'Are you going to finish school, Roy?'

'I hope to get my School Certificate. I don't know about after that.'

Mr O'Brien nods. He looks at Doyle. 'What's your advice to him, Mr Manager?'

'I think he should get his School Certificate and then we'll look at what his options are.'

'Well, that sounds like very good advice. You make a good pair. Doyle has the memory and Slaven's got the talent.' He then says, 'I've got a fair bit of silver beet here. Interested?'

Doyle and me look at each other and shrug. 'Wouldn't know what to do with it,' we say in unison. Mr O'Brien shakes his head. 'Thanks anyway, Mr O'Brien.'

O'Brien says he's been approached by the Shamrocks and the Workmen's Club and Oberon. I said Father Kane had mentioned playing with the Shammies, but I wasn't sure what I was going to do.

O'Brien added that the pool will be opening next week. Which means cricket training will be starting.

We ride off. We head through town and pass the church and ride through the pottery. We stop at the creek that runs through Sheedys Gully. Doyle tells me he can remember a particular day. The day before his fourth birthday. He said his family was living in Hassans Walls Road at the time and he walked out of the front yard and crossed the road and wandered through the bush all the way down to here. Half a mile. He pointed to the spot. 'I can remember lying by the creek dangling my arm in it. There were lots of birds. And lizards. Frogs. Lots of frogs. I must have been away for hours. Mum was out of her mind with worry. She thought I might have been abducted. She ran into Mrs Lewin's house next door where they had a phone and she called the police. And she called my Uncle Ray at Finley's.

'It was Uncle Ray who found me. I can see him walking towards me with a big smile on his face. White shirt, grey pants. A black belt with a silver buckle. No tie. Black shoes. Grey socks. He hoisted me into the air and sat me on his shoulders and we walked home. I wrapped my arms around his forehead, just as the goanna did with Sherb. There were two police cars parked outside our house and I can see Mum running across the street to Uncle Ray and me and she was in tears of rage, and she belted me across the legs and I had no idea why I was in so much trouble. It must have made her look like a bad mother or something.

'But she had a lot to be worried about. Jen was beginning to become strange, you know? Mum was massaging her continually for hours on end. Jen couldn't stand on her feet. There was no life in her eyes. Mum was panicking. She was reaching out in desperation, trying to save a daughter who she thought, she knew, she could see, was disappearing, was changing. I was fine. I would have come home. I knew where I was. Up 'til that point I was having just the best day. Can't remember a thing about my birthday.'

•

I went around to Doyle's that night. There was no drama with his sister. No incidents. No mad house. We sat in the beer room on the floor and drank Cokes. When his grandma went to bed we listened to *Rubber Soul* and we talked about what next year might be like. We agreed that we'd miss Mahon and Brewer and Brennan and Hall. It felt like the end of an era.

Toasted ham and mustard. Delicious. He'd cut the slices from the ham bone on the machine at the back of the shop. The cutting took seconds. The cleaning up, minutes. But it was worth it.

I rode home and lit the fire on the off-chance that Mum might get home at a normal hour. She didn't and I went to bed when the television stations stopped transmitting.

Chapter Twenty-one

'You're a right-handed Gary Sobers.'
PETER PHILPOTT, TEST CRICKETER

'This kid scares me, Harry.'
JOHN NEWCOMBE, TENNIS CHAMPION

The final week of school was pretty relaxed. Not much work was done. Harold told us stories of when he was working as a wool classer. It didn't sound very interesting. Dean brought a pack of cards to school and he and Doyle and Benson and me played euchre in Maths and English. Benson could wander the school and do whatever he liked. He wore a new pair of brown overalls. He smoked with impunity. His skin had cleared up and the dandruff had disappeared. He shuffled the cards with a flourish. Brother Connor enjoyed watching the game. He circled our desk, looked at all our cards. He offered unhelpful advice. 'Go alone, Dean. I would.'

The final day began with mass with the girls. Father Keogh told us what an exciting year 1968 was going to be for us. The problems with the new public address system had been solved. He told us to keep up our prayers during the holidays and to have a happy and holy Christmas. We were then all dismissed.

I walked with Barbara down to the café at the picture theatre and we played pinball together, arm in arm, just like Flynn and Vicki Westwood.

•

The first week of the holidays was mainly taken up with Mum working out my schedule. It started when Brother Michael dropped in. The first time a Brother had been in the house. He was all smiles and a bit nervous.

Mum was embarrassed because the house was really messy. The washing up wasn't done and there were bits of material everywhere, and dresses in various states of completion. We hadn't done a spring clean and the wall above the fireplace was black with soot. As was part of the ceiling. I'd left my dirty clothes on the floor, which Mum really hates. 'Roy! For God's sake, put your washing in the laundry. How many times have I got to tell you?' Two cupboard doors in the kitchen swung awkwardly, each on one hinge only. Wherever you looked something was either askew or dusty or grubby or just uncared for. Mum's flowers from the opening night of *The Boy Friend* were lying dead on a fruit box. Still in the cellophane, as they had been presented. Brother Michael didn't know where to look.

Mum and I gave each other a long glance because we both realised what the place must look like to outside eyes. It all just reinforced the 'she needs a man about the house' whispers that followed Mum whenever she was in town.

'Look, I won't hold you up. I'm just the messenger.' From his pocket he took out a few pages torn from a pad. 'Mrs Slaven, Brother Hugh insists you use the school phone to return these calls.' He handed the pages to Mum.

'You're in demand,' he said to me.

Mum said, 'Thank you, Brother,' as she read the messages.

He was keen to get going. 'Well, I'll leave you to it.' I ushered him to the door, leaving Mum reading.

I said, 'What are you doing for holidays?'

'Be here most of the time. So much curriculum work. We're building this from scratch. I hope to get to Mum's for Christmas. Just a few days.' He looked exhausted.

'Any time for tennis?'

'Always!' he said with a smile. And he hopped into the white school Valiant station wagon.

When I went back inside Mum and I looked at each other and said as one, 'We've got to clean this house.' And we laughed.

Mum picked up the flowers and threw them at me. I picked up my dirty clothes and threw them at her. Then I'm chasing her out into my room and she's squealing. She's a schoolgirl again. Then she screams. It had been the first time she'd been in my room in weeks. My room makes the lounge room look like the Finley's showroom.

John Doyle

She looks at me. 'You start here.' I nod. Then she shook her head. 'What must that lovely young man think of us?'

•

Mum had to phone the New South Wales Country Rugby League, the Australian Rugby League, the Saint George Rugby League Club, the New South Wales Cricket Association, the Mosman Cricket Club, the New South Wales Lawn Tennis Association and the Australian Tennis Association. Some of the messages Mum said were 'just too silly'.

There followed a really busy time. Mum couldn't believe it. A car came from Sydney to pick me up and take me to White City. Mum came as well. We drove over the mountains and then right through the city to Rushcutters Bay.

They treat us like royalty. There are some sandwiches without crusts and a 'morning tea service'. Mum is wearing a green satin dress and some of the men are looking at her. They gush. She looks like Hollywood. She winks at me.

Eventually we're introduced to a Mr Hopman and he takes me down to the dressing rooms where there's clothing and Volley sandshoes and a new racquet. I get dressed, and every-thing fits, and he takes me out onto the court and stands at the net with a bucket of balls and tells me what shot he wants. It's very easy. Then he said, 'Play the shot you want.' I top-spin them all. He puts the bucket down. 'Stay here, Roy,' he says.

276

A couple of minutes later he returns with a man he introduces as John Newcombe. He's not dressed for tennis but is casual. He grins at me. 'Harry says you've got something I've got to see.'

I shrug.

Harry gives John his racquet. 'Have a hit.'

John picks up a couple of balls and hits one to me, I hit it straight back to him and he to me and me to him and we could have gone on forever.

Harry says, 'Hit it where you want to, Roy.' I top-spin drive it straight into the corner.

'Jesus,' says John Newcombe. He grabs another ball from Harry's bucket and hits it to my backhand. With top-spin I drive it into the other corner of the court.

'Jesus Christ,' says John Newcombe. He looks at Harry. 'He doesn't change his grip.'

'I know,' says Harry.

'This kid scares me, Harry.'

'Me too.'

I've got to come back in January. For a week. I'll be billeted with one of the club members. Mum asks the driver if we can stop at Mark Foy's on the way home. 'Of course, Mrs Slaven.'

We walked about looking at stuff for about an hour. Mum loved the fabrics but couldn't afford anything. But she did buy some new pretty underwear. We both fell asleep in the back seat of the Ford Fairlane on the way home. My old clothes were in a bag.

•

Two days later and Mr White at the Small Arms Factory allows Mum another day off to accompany me to Sydney on the train. We arrive at Central and are met by Ian Craig, a former captain of the Australian test cricket team. He's very friendly and takes an instant liking to Mum. 'You couldn't possibly be this young man's mother?' He drives us over the Harbour Bridge in his Mark II Jaguar and we arrive at the Mosman Cricket Club.

Ian is keen to get down to business and within fifteen minutes of arriving, I'm padded up in the nets with five men bowling at me. Ian stands outside the nets behind me, just as Brian Booth had done. I don't make the mistake of being too aggressive, and let any ball I don't need to play go by. Pretty quickly I'm reading the body language of the bowlers – the leg spinner, Peter Philpott, in particular. I read his wrong'un as it leaves his hand and deposit it over the oval fence behind his head.

He comes down to me with a big grin on his face. 'You picked that, didn't you?'

I nod.

'How?'

'Your left foot is wider on the crease.'

'Is it?'

Ian says, 'Word's going to get out, Percy.'

I bat for about an hour. No one gets me out. I stand about with the bowlers while Ian Craig talks to Mum.

Peter Philpott says he loves the way I bat. 'Beautiful to watch, son. It's effortless. You're a right-handed Gary Sobers. You don't bowl as well, do you?' I say no and he says, 'Thank God for that.' And he laughs. The other bowlers do as well.

'Who's your coach?'

'Mum is.'

'Bullshit.'

'True.'

We all have a cup of tea and lamingtons and it seems to me that Peter Philpott and two of the other bowlers are trying to crack onto Mum. She parries their banter and quite enjoys the attention. Peter Philpott gives Mum his number and says, 'If ever you're in Sydney and at a loose end, give me a call. We could go up Australia Square Tower and then to the Chevron Hilton for a drink and a talk. About cricket.'

Mum takes the number, puts it in her purse and says, 'I'll think about that.'

Ian Craig drives us back to Central well in time for the four-thirty train back to Lithgow. He tells us that he was very young when he started playing first-class cricket and cricket is 'a simply marvellous way of seeing the world'.

On the train home, Mum says, 'I don't know what I'm going to do about you, Roy. You're going to have to leave Lithgow.'

I panic a bit and shake my head. 'I'm never leaving you, Mum.'

'Oh, you won't be leaving me for a while yet.' And she leans over and kisses me on the forehead. 'I'm very proud of you. You could so easily be a show-off. But you're not.'

We both loved riding in the Jaguar. We loved the Harbour Bridge. We loved seeing the big beautiful houses in Mosman. We hated Sydney, though.

After a while Mum rests her head against the carriage window and together we daydream as night begins to fall, and we can taste the sweetness of the mountain air once more.

•

A letter arrives from a Mr Frank Facer, who is the boss of the Saint George Rugby League Club. It said that, 'On the strength of the recommendations from Mr Ron Livermore and Mr Barry Slaven, we are offering a contract to Roy Patrick Slaven for the sum of two hundred and fifty dollars, annually, until he turns eighteen, at which time Roy Patrick Slaven will agree to sign as a player with the Saint George Rugby League Club.' He is calling it a scholarship. A cheque from the Commonwealth Bank is attached to the legal agreement.

Mum is overwhelmed. 'Oh my God, Roy. What is going on here? Two hundred and fifty dollars! Look at that. It's the biggest cheque I have ever seen.' She uses the contract as a fan to cool her face as she paces the lounge room. 'I'll have to ask Ross Higgins to have a look at it.' Mum is very distracted. 'I'll have that dress for your Barbara finished tomorrow,' she says.

'Great, Mum. She's been away for a couple of weeks. She's back on Saturday. We could buy a car.' I leave Mum pondering. She knows a car is possible. Mum could drive.

I saw Doyle when I was getting cornflakes, tomato sauce and sausages in town. He's got some holiday work with his Uncle Ray at Finley's. He invited me around to his place. I get there at about eight thirty. His mum and dad have gone to the mountains to watch Tony Doyle's band. His eldest sister Deanna is over from Bathurst. It's a different atmosphere. The television is off. Grandma sits on a dining chair with a two-year-old boy awkwardly cradled in her arms. Cath is sitting in a lounge chair not wanting to be noticed in case she's told to go to bed. Deanna is a fair bit younger than Mum. She's nothing like Doyle at all. She's blonde and really pretty. And she laughs a lot. 'You're the boy who beat the man. I love tennis.'

Doyle tells her that I've met Harry Hopman and hit balls with John Newcombe. Just this week.

'Oh, yeah? Is that right?' She doesn't believe him.

'I can't hold him any longer,' says Grandma and Deanna scoops the little boy up in her arms. 'That's okay, Ma. Do you want me to turn the television on?'

'Yes,' she says as she struggles to her feet.

Deanna asks, 'What are you boys up to tonight?'

'Coke and chocolate in the beer room.'

'Well, Coke and chocolate in the beer room sounds pretty good to me. Have you done the milk crates?' Doyle nods. 'Good on you, love. Bugger of a job. I'd better put this little man down. Nice to meet you, Roy.' She goes through one of the doors into a part of the house I have never seen.

Doyle and I go down into the shop and grab a Coke and Doyle suggests a Fry's dark chocolate and peppermint bar.

In the beer room I tell him about the offer from Saint George and the trip on the train to Sydney with Mum. He wants to know how quick the bowlers were. I said faster than Horner. I said one bloke was getting the shits with me and dropped it short, but I could see it coming and just ducked. All that effort for nothing. Bowlers aren't smart. Peter Philpott was nice, though. Hard to score off.

We hear Jen shouting. Doyle ignores it. He says Deanna is much better with Jen than he is. The shouting doesn't last long.

Doyle plays on his tape recorder a recording he has made of himself speaking. He calls it a 'radio play'. He speaks as a man who's lying in bed in the dark trying to get to sleep and keeps hearing things. He whispers to himself 'What's that? Did you hear that? A scratching. A mouse? A cat?' Silence. 'There it is again. It sounds like a man. A man with a knife.' Then there's a lot of silence. 'Surely you heard that. Surely.' Silence. 'The cocking of a gun. No. A pistol. With a silencer. That's what it is.' Silence.

It's not very entertaining. He sees my impatience. He stops the tape. 'He's a victim of his imagination.' I nod. 'I think it's funny. He just keeps imagining things. Things that frighten him. And we, as an audience, know that there is nothing there.' I nod. 'It's funny,' he repeats.

I try to offer encouragement, but I can't see people gathering around the radio to listen. He's about to play some more, and

I'm relieved when Deanna pokes her head in. She's brought some 'ears of corn' from Bathurst. We go into the kitchen and she serves up the hot corn smeared with butter and pepper. We pick it up with our hands and eat it. It's the first time I have ever eaten real corn. It's really tasty. I ask her how she's cooked it, thinking I could surprise Mum with it if I could get some somewhere. She gives me four ears from a basket and instructs me to strip off the outer layers and boil it in salty water for about five minutes and that's it. 'Couldn't be simpler,' she says.

Grandma goes to bed. 'You shouldn't be eating at this time of night.'

'You're right there, Ma,' says Deanna.

'And that child should be in bed.'

Deanna goes into the lounge room. 'Cath! Are you still up? Get to bed this minute.'

She reluctantly takes herself off to bed.

Doyle makes us all a cup of Nestlés Quik and he and I stand in the backyard looking at the full moon through his telescope. He says it's better with a half-moon, the craters are more obvious. I think the moon looks close enough to touch. Doyle says the Americans were hoping to get a man on the moon soon and that his grandma thought he was making it up. He says he's hoping she'll live long enough for him to prove her wrong.

Deanna came out and had a look. She couldn't believe how quickly it was moving.

Chapter Twenty-two

'You can take the boy out of Lithgow, but you
can never take Lithgow out of the boy.'
STEPHEN 'SPUD' MURPHY

I decided to make Mum a special breakfast in bed. I found a wide piece of planed wood in the backyard that Dad had discarded when making the furniture for the house and covered it with a pillowcase. I used it as a tray. I delivered to Mum a cooked ear of corn with butter and pepper, and scrambled eggs on toast with a cup of tea. She had just woken up.

She sat up, pushed pillows behind her back and told me she loved me. She was excited. 'Breakfast in bed! My God! I am so spoilt.' I left her to it and turned the television on and had mine.

'I love this corn!' Mum shouted from the bedroom. Then, 'I love scrambled eggs!' Then, 'I think I have created the world's most wonderful man!' She was happy. So was I. There was nothing interesting on Channel Nine. I switched to the ABC. It was worse.

•

I see Barbara at the eight-thirty mass and tell her the dress Mum's made for her is ready. We agree I'll drop it in to her in the afternoon. It's pretty risky because she hasn't had a fitting. I'm too embarrassed to ask her over to my place. Even though we've cleaned it up, it still looks a bit ordinary.

I knock on her door, she lets me in and we climb the stairs to her 'home in the sky', as she calls it. It wouldn't suit me, having no backyard, but having stairs is exciting. The ceilings are really high and ornate. It is spotlessly clean and really comfortable. Furniture like in Finley's. She's home by herself, so I can relax. Her dad scares me a bit.

She disappears into her bedroom and returns wearing the new item. It's a powder blue Dacron dress that sits a few inches above the knee. It fits perfectly and she loves it. She looks a million dollars and I tell her as much. We kiss. We really kiss. Our tongues find each other's. Our tongues explore. I eke out every aspect of her mouth. It is exhilarating. We stare at each other. We are both breathing heavily. Her face is pale. Mine probably is too. There are very strong feelings gathering. We kiss again. With just as much passion. My hands move around her back. I'm reaching down to her buttock. I think she feels my arousal. I see her bedroom door is open. I see the foot of her bed, and then, I think of what Mum said to me.

'Have you ever climbed Scotsman's Hill?' I say.

She looks at me and takes this in. This is a real change in direction.

'Dressed like this?'

'I just thought . . .'

She looks at her watch. 'I haven't climbed it. Is it worth it?'

'Best view in the world, some say.'

She can see it is a good idea. 'I'll get changed.' And five minutes later, she's changed into blue jeans, white shirt, sensible shoes and has left a note for her dad, and we're walking hand in hand down Main Street towards the viaduct. We bump into Flynn and Vicki Westwood, walking hand in hand towards us. They've been playing pinball. We tell them of our plans. The climb.

Flynn would love to come. Vicki Westwood is not interested in the slightest. 'Shit a brick. That's a really stupid thing to do.'

'The view is great,' says Flynn.

'You go then.'

He weighs it up. He looks at us and, being Flynn, is sensitive enough to know that he'd be a spare dick at a wedding. They stick with their plan of watching television at Vicki Westwood's place. She has a twenty-six inch screen. The biggest in Lithgow. And she's a big fan of *Roller Games*. We stick to our plan. We part.

We talk about how much we'd like to see Vicki Westwood's television set. Barbara only gets Channel Two. She's never seen *Peyton Place* or *Voyage to the Bottom of the Sea* or *Star Trek* or . . .

she'd seen no ads! She said Deirdre had told her all about the ads and the shows and she didn't really think she'd missed out on too much. I knew she was wrong. I told her she was wrong.

'Do you watch *Z-Cars*?'

'What's that?' I said.

'*Bellbird*?'

'What's that?'

'*Maigret*?'

She was speaking a foreign language. I told her I have trouble with the ABC because there are no ads. It's dull. She said she thought I was missing out. I told her I knew she was missing out. We stopped walking. We kissed. I said I'd watch *Z-Cars*. She said I'd really like it.

•

I watched *Z-Cars* with Mum a week or so later. Dull. Real dull. Mum thought the acting was really good. I didn't tell Barbara I thought it was dull.

•

I'm not sure how much Barbara enjoyed the climb. 'How much further?' was a frequent question. And she had to be assisted getting over and through a couple of the awkward rock outcrops that blocked the path. Sometimes we'd find ourselves turning assistance into a cuddle. She needed a few breaks to catch her breath. It took forty minutes.

I wrap my hands over her eyes and steer her towards the edge of a huge perfectly flat sandstone boulder at the very apex of Scotsman's Hill.

I take my hands away and she is stunned.

'Thank you for this,' she says. She is genuinely excited. We sit on the edge. Dangle our legs. There is no smoke. No clouds. The sun is strong and the air is dry and the clarity is perfect. Things are both close and far away. And the things far away are just as clear as the things up close. She drinks it in.

After a couple of minutes of total silence, we work out her route to De La Salle from home. I show her where I live. We can see our new antenna. I show her where Doyle lives and where Dean lives and where Brewer lives. She shows me where Deirdre lives and where Margot lives and where Anne and Marilyn and the Cullen girls live. I tell her that Doyle and Dean think this was once part of the sea floor. There are shells in the rocks. Brother Michael came up with us once and he agreed.

Barbara nods. She thinks about it. 'What happened to all the water?'

I think about it. 'Good question.' Then I remember Doyle talking to Brother Michael about it. 'Tectonic forces. Uplift. Or something. Over millions of years.'

She looks unconvinced. Then she says, 'Sister Geraldine likes that sort of stuff. I suppose it's interesting. Not so much to me. I'm more interested in the present.'

I nod.

'And the future.'

I nod. 'So am I.'

I ask her advice. I tell her all about meeting Ian Craig and Harry Hopman and the offer from Saint George. She has never heard of Ian Craig or Harry Hopman but realises they must be important. I tell her about Sydney and the Harbour Bridge and the millions of houses and people. How high Australia Square Tower is. The shelves in the Jaguar. The smell of the Jaguar. How quiet it was. Some of the shots I'd played against John Newcombe. The tea service. Small sandwiches with the crusts cut off. How great a bloke Peter Philpott was. Doyle's idea of playing snooker in the clubs. How well I can see things. Sensing the beauty of nature and the colour of the sky when we played the grand final against High School. Seeing a Regent honeyeater and knowing what it was. How Doyle goes around cursing God in his mind and having to confess to having had these thoughts to priests in the dark and he's thinking bad thoughts about God while he's actually confessing.

Lots of stuff came out. Breaking my nose. Mum's torpedo pass. The goanna on Sherb's head. Being called 'Bot's boy'. How much I resented Dad, and the number of people who hate him. How much better it was at home without him. I was gabbling at times, tumbling over words. Mixing stories up. I told her I asked Doyle to be my manager and, as I said it, realised he had told me he was going to be my manager. So I had to correct that.

Getting confused. Making corrections. It's the most I have ever said to anyone. I think I'm starting to sound like Brian Lawson. I stop talking.

Barbara looks at me squarely. 'Doyle's your best friend, isn't he?'

I look at her. It hadn't occurred to me to rank friends. 'Best friend?' I say. She nodded. 'I think Mum's my best friend. And would I rather be here with you than sitting with Doyle in his beer room? Well, there's no contest. But he'd be third. He attacks life like he attacks the new ball. With fear, panic and trepidation. I think he needs me.'

Barbara considers all of this.

I go on. 'Just as I can read the ball leaving the bowler's hand, he can read the foibles in people. It's his sport. It's not a very useful skill, I don't reckon.'

We sit together silently. Magpies call and answer. The angle of the sun causes Mount Walker to glow. The sandstone curtains of Hassans Walls are turning deep ochre. The town is glowing and at rest. She said she'd been to Sydney once. Stanmore. Last year. She could never imagine living there. It was far too busy. Too many people. No sense of space. Too ugly. Too chaotic. She wants to live her life in Lithgow.

Looking out, it seemed like paradise to me. I'd be happy to never leave. I told her as much.

She said I must be under a lot of pressure. She put her arm around me. She says the whole town is talking about me. 'How does that feel? Being talked about.'

'Dunno, Barb.'

I'm about to say something else, but we look at each other. We realise that was the first time I had called her 'Barb'. She smiles.

'But never Barbie, okay? I hate Barbie. Lennan called me Barbie at the social.'

I remembered Lennan dancing with her. 'You know, if I was Doyle,' I say, 'I'd start calling you Barbie right now.'

'You're not Doyle. Thank God. I never know whether he's being serious or making fun of me.'

I was really tempted to call her Barbie. The devil in me, I suppose.

I realised that Doyle probably has the devil in him. He'd be calling her Barbie for the rest of her life.

She doesn't know what advice to give me. 'It seems to me that you can do whatever you want to do. And it's doing what you love doing. Playing sport. I wouldn't be complaining. You've been kissed by a rainbow, Dad says.'

This pleases me. I so want to win him over without the need of O'Brien's father.

She says, 'Saint George is a strong club, isn't it?'

'The strongest.'

I tell her I'm not sure how I can play cricket and tennis at the same time.

'Well, what a cross to bear. Poor you.'

I smile at her. She is right. She smiles back. I put my arm around her. We look out across the valley. The friendly sunny girl, and the boy friend, sitting together, on the very top of our world.

It's a bit harder for Barb to climb down than it was going up. She slips quite a bit, grazes her elbow and is grateful when we finally reach the road at the base of the hill.

'It was worth it. The view made me feel like I was flying. Thank you. I'd love to show Deirdre but she'd never do it. Pat might. But, to be realistic, I can't see myself ever going up there again. Coming down is the hardest. You didn't tell me that.'

'Sorry about that. I forgot.'

We amble back. It's dusk. We're hand in hand, boyfriend and girlfriend. I think it's official. We stroll through the viaduct and up Main Street to her sky home. 'Please thank your mum for the beautiful dress. And promise me you won't tell Doyle I hate "Barbie".'

I promise.

We part with a kiss. It's long. Tongues are involved. There is so much to explore.

I kept my promise. I didn't tell Doyle.

•

Mum is really pleased Barbara's dress fits her so well. She has spoken to Mr Higgins and the offer from Saint George is above board. She's put the cheque into her bank account.

'Mr Higgins said you've got to get him the autographs of Reg Gasnier and Graeme Langlands and Johnny Raper.'

I nod.

'And he wants your autograph.' Then she says, 'Uncle Baz and Aunty Rita have invited us to Cowra for Christmas.'

John Doyle

This is the best news.

'Can we go, Mum? I love Uncle Baz.'

'Of course we're going. We need a holiday. And guess what? I've bought us a car.'

It's a blue and cream HB Holden. It's only got thirty-two thousand miles on it. It looks magnificent in the backyard, beside the bags and the coal heap. It even has a radio.

Mum takes me for a drive. We smile at each other. We drive out along Marrangaroo and Mum turns off into what I discover is the Lithgow Golf Club. We enter the car park beside the clubhouse and pull up by a notice board. It has the rates for club hire and the dress code in bold black letters.

'You've never played golf, have you, love?'

'Never.'

'Some of the girls come here on Saturday nights. The Murphy brothers play here.'

'They live in O'Brien's street. I've met Spud.' Mum nods. She looks at the large clubhouse and shakes her head.

'The only blokes I know in Lithgow who play golf are the really dull ones. Your father played golf.'

'Yeah?'

'He was pretty good. Baz might still have his old golf clubs. You could play a round or two in Cowra if you like.'

I nod. Sounds good to me. Then Mum looks at me again. 'On second thoughts, I don't think it's a good idea, Roy. You'll be really good at it and break some sort of record and then

294

we'll have golfing people bearing down on us. Trips to Sydney to meet . . . Kel someone.'

'Nagle. Kel Nagle.'

Mum laughs. 'Yeah. Kel Nagle. And what am I going to talk to Kel Nagle about? "Nice cardigan, Kel. Nice hat".' She laughs again.

'I'm putting my foot down, Roy. Under no circumstances are you to touch your father's golf clubs. There will be no discussion entered into.' Another laugh.

'Now you're sounding like Brother Connor.'

'Well. He might be mad. Maureen. I rest my case. But he gets results. You passed Maths.'

Mum negotiates the tricky pot-filled road that joins the golf club to the highway. She's a really good driver. Taught by her brothers, two of them race cars for a living. Her father, the granddad I've never met, was a mechanic. Might still be.

We head back to town. The sun is setting. The honey-coloured light causes the hills to glow. There is no traffic. A train passes over the viaduct. Mum suggests we get a hamburger for tea from The Classic. With chips. Sounds good to me.

I put the car radio on. 2LT. 'Friday on My Mind'. Mum taps the steering wheel.

Lithgow in 1968 was just around the corner.

God, I was happy.

Doyle being a crawler in fourth class.

The 1968 class photo with Brother Hugh. Flynn is sitting in the front row, third from the left, and beside him on the right is Barbara. Doyle's there too, third from the right up the back.

The school captains in front of Mr Goggin's shelves: Julie, Beth, Margot and Barbara in the back row, and Marsland, Dean, Lennan, Doyle and O'Brien in the front. Crawlers, all.

Acknowledgements

I would like to thank copyeditor Deonie Fiford for her diligence in compensating for my laziness.

I would like to thank the staff of the Lithgow Public Library for their courtesy and efficiency, the De La Salle Brothers for giving me the understanding of the word 'vocation', and the Catholic Church for giving me the word 'sodality'.

And my old friends for allowing me to remember them.

And my family.